ALBERT CAMUS

ALBERT CAMUS

THE THINKER, THE ARTIST, THE MAN

STEPHEN ERIC BRONNER

Frontis: Albert Camus by Henri Cartier-Bresson

© 1996 Stephen Eric Bronner
All rights reserved.
Published simultaneously in Canada
Franklin Watts, a Division of Grolier Publishing Co., Inc.

Bronner, Stephen Eric, 1949–
Albert Camus: the thinker, the artist, the man/Stephen Eric Bronner.
p. cm.
Includes bibliographical references and index.
Summary: A biography of the Algerian-born,
French existential novelist, dramatist, and essayist.
ISBN 0–531–11305–1
1. Camus, Albert, 1913–1960—Biography—Juvenile literataure.
2. Authors, French—20th century—Biography—Juvenile literature.
[1. Camus, Albert, 1913–1960. 2. Authors, French. 3. Authors, Algerian.]
I. Title.
PQ2605.A3734Z6255 1996
848'.91409—dc20
[B]   96–18965
                                                          CIP
                                                           AC

Printed in the United States of America
1 2 3 4 5 6 7 8 9 10 R 05 04 03 02 01 00 99 98 97 96

CONTENTS

To Alexander Eric Lanigan

ALBERT CAMUS

1

ALGERIA

ALBERT CAMUS, BORN ON NOVEMBER 7, ~~1912~~, WOULD *1913* become a man of two continents. Algeria, unlike other colonies in the French empire, was always considered part of France especially by its white settlers, or *pied-noirs*. French settlers, many from Alsace-Lorraine, had moved to the north African colony following the Franco-Prussian War of 1871.[1] Much of Camus' thinking and many of his values become more comprehensible in the light of this French-Algerian heritage.

Albert was only a year old when his father, Lucien, died at the age of twenty-nine at the Battle of the Marne, one of the bloodiest in World War I. Lucien Auguste Camus had also lost his father at the age of one, after which his four older brothers and sisters placed him in an orphanage. Lucien taught himself to read and write and, after running away from the orphanage, became an apprentice in a vineyard in the Algerian town of Cheraga. There he met his future wife, Catherine Sintés.

The young people were soon separated. Lucien Auguste was drafted in 1906 and spent the next two years

11

performing military service in Casablanca, Morocco. During this period Catherine moved with her family to the Belcourt section of Algiers.

Upon his discharge, Lucien Camus refused to reconcile with his siblings. Instead Lucien Auguste and Catherine married in 1909 and, in 1910, a son, Lucien Camus, was born. Work with a wine company led the father to settle the family near the little village of Mondavi where Albert Camus was born. With the outbreak of World War I the father rejoined the army and was killed in 1914.

Albert Camus had few memories of his father, but he would always remain close to his brother, Lucien. His mother would figure prominently in his first collection of essays and in his anguished reflections on the Algerian War. Catherine, who was of Spanish origin, was one of nine children whose ancestors had migrated to Algeria in 1850. She was deaf and illiterate and suffered from a speech impediment caused by an untreated illness during her childhood.

Without any resources, following the death of her husband, she moved back to the home of her deeply religious mother in the working-class neighborhood of Belcourt. Catherine and the two young children shared a three-room apartment with her mother and her two older brothers Joseph and Etienne. Joseph left in 1920 to build a life of his own. Etienne was born mute and, after an operation at the age of thirteen, could only speak with difficulty. He worked at a cooperage that built barrels. Catherine, although receiving a small widows' pension, cleaned houses in order to make ends meet. Both Catherine and Etienne were subservient to their domineering mother who was known to discipline her grandchildren with a whip. This bleak existence is described by Albert Camus:

There were five of them living together: the grandmother, her younger son, her elder daughter, and the daughter's two children. The son was almost dumb; the daughter, an invalid, could only think with difficulty; and of the two children, one was already working for an insurance company while the other was continuing his studies. At seventy, the grandmother still dominated all these people. . . . With enormous clear, cold eyes, she had a regal posture, that she relinquished only with increasing age, but which she still sometimes tried to recover when she went out. [2]

The poverty in which Camus grew to maturity was both material and emotional. There were no books at home. His grandmother and mother never joked or chatted for his mother had difficulty speaking and hearing; they were fatalistic, pessimistic, and stoical. The uncle didn't help matters. The gloomy atmosphere was compounded by economic want. "A certain number of years lived without money," Camus could write, "are enough to create a whole sensibility." [3]

Moments of happiness were savored. Camus never really complained about his impoverished childhood. He eloquently stated that for all the poverty he witnessed in Algeria, it could not compare with the cold, gray slums of Europe. His early experiences gave him the ability in later life to speak with people from all classes. His childhood taught him a singular understanding of misery, which made his empathy with the disempowered genuine. The racially mixed character of Belcourt, with its Jews and Europeans and Muslims, [4] also provided Camus with a cosmopolitan outlook and inspired a hatred of intolerance, especially the arrogance and racism of the French toward the Arabs.

His childhood, undeniably, left scars. He would always feel the need to prove himself, with women as well as with work, and he often indulged in acting tough. Jean Grenier, a teacher and friend of Camus, noted that "his

Albert Camus' First Communion portrait

adolescence was accompanied by a general contempt for the entire world and a will to personal domination."[5] The tension experienced by Camus during childhood produced two opposing attitudes: exhilaration and optimism coupled with bitterness and pessimism.

The relations between Camus and his teachers partially compensated for the emotional emptiness he experienced at home. As the child of a fallen soldier, a *pupille de la nation*, he received a small allowance for school supplies from the state. From the age of five to ten (1918 to 1923) he attended public school. In his last year at the school, a teacher, Louis Germain—to whom he would later dedicate his acceptance speech for the Nobel Prize for Literature—recognized his talent and took a liking to him. Germain helped Camus, who was a model student, win a high school scholarship in 1924 to the *Grand Lycée* (high school). For the next seven years, until 1931, Camus attended the high school. Germain was apparently a man of liberal principles,[6] like so many others of the teaching profession, and he undoubtedly helped instill a respect for basic democratic values in his prize pupil. On receiving the Nobel prize in 1957, Camus wrote a letter to Germain, which beautifully expressed his feelings:

When I heard the news, my first thought, after my mother, was of you. Without you, without the affectionate hand you extended to the small poor child that I was, without your teaching, and your example, none of all this would have happened. But at least it gives me an opportunity to tell you what you have been and still are for me, and to assure you that your efforts, your work, and the generous heart you put into it still live in one of your little schoolboys who, despite the years, has never stopped being your grateful pupil.[7]

Despite his enthusiasm for school, however, the interest of the young Camus was also directed to soccer and, as he

*Albert Camus (in black, seated on the bench) in his
uncle's workshop*

grew a bit older, to hanging around Algiers with his friends from the neighborhood. "Innocence" was the word he used to describe his youth. Things changed in 1930, however, when he learned he was suffering from tuberculosis. He spent a year recuperating with the family of his uncle Gustave Acault, a self-educated man who worked as a butcher. The next year he spent studying for his baccalaureate, which he received in 1932. Acault had befriended his nephew earlier and helped introduce him to modern literature. Ultimately, Acault was a model for Meursault, the main character in the novel, *The Stranger (L'Etranger)*.

Nineteen thirty was also the year in which Camus met the man who would exert the most profound influence on his career: Jean Grenier.[8] As Camus' high school philosophy teacher, he introduced him to the world of ideas as well as to the thinking of Henri Bergson and Friedrich Nietzsche. Grenier was the author of the essay collections, *Islands* (1933) and *Mediterranean Inspirations* (1941). A passionate democrat and a committed teacher, Grenier had left France for Algeria in order to experience a culture different than that of mainland France. A friend of famous writers like André Malraux and André Gide, whom he met while working briefly for the publishing house of Gallimard and writing for the prestigious *Nouvelle Revue Française*, Grenier viewed European civilization as decadent. He contrasted it with the earlier vitality of Greek literature and philosophy beginning with Plato. Through his teaching and writings, he provided his student with an exhilirating insight into the "pagan" influence of Greece, and a source of renewal in what Camus would later call the "Mediterranean temperament."

Grenier also affected the art of Camus. *Islands*, which was composed of fragments of experience, inspired the

Albert Camus (seated cross-legged in front)
with his soccer team, circa 1930

style of two essay collections and Camus' choice of themes. Its "pagan" preoccupation with sensuality and natural beauty, which contrasted so starkly with the rationalizing forces of "civilization," influenced Camus as surely as had Grenier's emphasis on loneliness and death. In Grenier's view people are stranded on deserted islands, lonely, bereft of religious hope, and without philosophical answers to the deepest questions on the meaning of life. Like the future writings of his pupil, those of Grenier blend a classical simplicitly of form with romantic accounts of personal experience.

A preoccupation with death also bound the two. Grenier saw death as simultaneously rounding out human existence and creating an "amputated being" or a life always cut short. His notion must have profoundly affected Camus when the young man, having learned of his tuberculosis, was forced to confront his mortality in a new way.[9] When combined with the Catholicism inherited from a deeply religious mother, this looming presence of death helps explain the obsession with God and theological questions that would remain with Camus throughout his life.

In 1932, the same year he received his graduation degree from the *Grand Lycée*, Camus met Simone Hié. Issues of personal responsibility, fate, and meaning surely assumed added importance following his disastrous marriage to Simone Hié. A year younger than Camus, she was, by all accounts, a talented actress and extraordinary beauty. A bohemian and a nonconformist, the daughter of a noted radical doctor, she had become addicted to morphine around the age of fourteen. She was a captivating woman and well liked among the young people of Algiers. Simone was engaged to one of Camus' best friends, Max-Pol Fouchét, a leader of the Federation of Young Socialists in Algeria, when she met Camus. Soon enough, however, she transferred her affections from Fouchet to Camus, and the friendship between the young men ended.

The Acaults, with whom Camus was still living, disapproved of Simone and thought that their nephew's intention of marrying her was an enormous mistake. Arguments between Gustave and Albert grew more frequent and more heated. Camus finally left the Acaults and moved in briefly with his brother Lucien. With financial support from his future mother-in-law and the wages he earned tutoring high school students, Camus began studying philosophy full-time at the University of Algiers in 1933.

In 1934 Camus and Simone were married. Things went well at first. They traveled and even attended classes together. Soon, however, their relationship became dominated by her morphine habit. Unsuccessful attempts to overcome her addiction were coupled with stratagems to maintain her habit. She exchanged sex with her doctors for drugs. Camus was mortified. Initially, he believed he could cure his wife. But he was wrong. Her condition gradually deteriorated. She became more erratic. She often embarrassed him in public and seduced his friends. They drifted apart and by 1935 Camus was no longer living with her. They didn't bother to divorce, however, until Camus decided to marry Francine Faure, in 1940. But his affection remained for Simone, who died in 1970, and, during the ensuing years, he complied whenever she requested money for her addiction.

During this difficult period Camus became interested in the theater and the world of left-wing politics. In 1935 he founded a theater troupe, the Workers Theater, and wrote several plays for the troupe. Also in 1935, or perhaps earlier, he joined the French Communist party in Algiers. About this time, Camus met two young students—Jeanne-Paul Sicard and Marguerite Dobrenn—with whom he would remain close friends until the end of his life. Both were members of the Communist party in their youth and interested in theater; both moved toward General Charles de Gaulle during the Resistance; both became important political functionaries in the postwar era; and both, for a few years beginning in 1935, shared a residence with Camus high above Algiers. He called this refuge the House at the Edge of the World.

Grenier took a post of professor at the University of Algiers when Camus enrolled in 1933. Their relationship continued as Camus wrote the thesis for his diploma, which he received in 1936. It is a difficult text. Nevertheless, "Christian Metaphysics and Neoplatonism" provides insight into the issue of Camus' relation to religion.

The thesis examined the way Christianity gradually embraced Hellenism, or the ideals of ancient Greece. The issue is of some importance since rational knowledge and worldly experience, which constitute basic elements of the Hellenic legacy, seemingly stand in stark opposition to the emphasis placed on revealed faith and the inner life by Christian religion. These conflicting tendencies—between the rational and experience of the inner life—manifest themselves in all of Camus' later writings.

It is noteworthy that the two most prominent philosophers discussed in his thesis, Plotinus and St. Augustine, were both of North African origin. Of particular interest is the way in which the dissertation justifies the use of language to convey the most deeply personal forms of experience and his interpretation of Plotinus, the third-century philosopher, who had originally seen language as a way of clarifying religious revelation.

The neoplatonism of Plotinus rested on belief in a cosmological connection between God and the world. This was embraced by St. Augustine in his famous *Confessions*, the first self-conscious autobiography. In its pages Camus saw the possibility of personal experience becoming the "constant point of reference for a literary and philosophical undertaking." In fact, the two genres merge in this great work of St. Augustine, just as in the writings of Camus.

The *Confessions*, which was obviously fueled by intense reflection, assumed a natural desire for God on the part of every person. Camus accepted this idea even though he already considered himself an atheist when he wrote "Christian Metaphysics and Neoplatonism." He ultimately combined the idea of the absence of God with the concept of a natural longing for salvation and meaning that only God can provide. This paradoxical situation would define the "absurd" character of existence, and inform all of Camus' future writings.[10]

★ ★ ★ ★ ★

Camus was neither a closet Catholic nor a secular thinker who, like Voltaire, considered religion little more than "superstition." Camus was actually representative of a philosophical trend known as "religious atheism." Its artistic and philosophical proponents were all intellectuals like Nietzsche, Martin Heidegger, and Karl Jaspers. They belonged to no church, embraced no religious dogma, and founded no mass movement. All of them emphasized the role of personal experience, however, and sought to counter the "emptiness" of modern philosophical traditions and the inner poverty caused by modern science and commodity production—what Max Weber termed the "disenchantment of the world." Thus, even if many of its major representatives were atheists or agnostics, God was the point of philsophical reference.

These are the terms in which Camus would formulate his philosophy. The "absurd" exists because God is absent. This means issues of religion have been taken seriously. Camus reflected the cultural concerns of his age. His own preoccupation with an absolute provided the context for investigating new problems, both existential and political.

2

PRELUDES

A HAPPY DEATH, (UNE MORTE HEUREUSE), CAMUS'
first novel, was written sometime between 1936 and 1938
when Camus was working as a journalist and performing
odd jobs, but it was not published until 1971. Its title
inverted that of *The Happy Life*, the first philosophical
effort of St. Augustine, and it contested the old saying:
"money can't buy happiness." Its hero, Patrice Mersault,
suffers from tuberculosis. He exhibits a lassitude and
indifference toward existence. He is only driven to self-
conscious action when his former teacher, a legless
cripple named Zagreus, complains of being forced to
await a "natural death."

Repulsed by the fate in store for his former mentor,
and tempted by his money, Mersault shoots Zagreus,
makes it look like suicide, and robs him in the hope of
securing a happy life. Camus was obviously seeking to
work through the central contradiction of St. Augustine's
The Happy Life. There it becomes apparent that, even
though no one can be happy who does not have what he

The city of Algiers viewed from the sea

or she desires, a person may have what is desired and still not be happy. St. Augustine, of course, was seeking to emphasize the primacy of faith over the search for truth or earthly pleasure. Camus wants to argue the opposite. But he is not quite certain how to proceed and, following the murder, the story begins to disintegrate.

Mersault wanders through central Europe, but the grayness depresses him. He longs for the sun and returns to Algiers where he happily shares a residence with three young women, remarkably similar to the House at the Edge of the World, and marries another. In the end, unrepentant, Mersault dies of tuberculosis. A "pagan" sensualism is the response to a fallen and decadent Christian world in *A Happy Death*. There is no salvation and no "tomorrow." There are experiences of joy. Even the beauty of nature, however, cannot compensate for the existence of injustice or the certainty of death.[1]

A parallel emerges with *The Stranger* (*L' Etranger*) for which *A Happy Death* served as a dress rehearsal. Its hero has marked similarities and virtually the identical name as the protagonist of the later work. Both novels are set in Algeria and deal with similar themes. A murder takes place in both, though in *A Happy Death*, Zagreus, rather than a nameless Arab, is the victim. Both novels also oscillate between pessimism and optimism. It was the same with Camus himself. Just like his atheism, which took shape in opposition to Catholicism, each of these two mutually exclusive views of life became defined by the other. This was also true of two other works written at th same time.

The Right Side and the Wrong Side (*L'Envers et l'Endroit*), a collection of essays and sketches, was published in 1937 in a limited edition by Charlot, a small publishing house, and a second collection, *Nuptials* (*Les Noces*), appeared two years later. With great hesitancy, Camus consented to their republication in 1958. He must have been somewhat ambivalent about their auto-biographical character; indeed, the 1958 preface to *The Right Side and the Wrong Side* could note: "here are my people, my teachers, my ancestry; here is what, through them, links me with everyone."[2]

Some essays such as "Between Yes and No" exhibit a self-pitying and emotionally effusive quality foreign to his more mature works. Others, such as "Summer in Algiers," tend to romanticize working-class life. At their best, however, these sketches of momentary experiences and everyday life combine romantic and sensual content with a classical form for which Camus would become known.

Both collections express the same tension. Outside is the sun, the sea, and physical experience. Inside is isolation, bitter poverty, cramped quarters, and a stultifying silence. Camus stands between the two, slipping from the one into the other, flipping the two sides of the coin back and forth, as the title of the first collection—*L'Envers et l'Endroit*—suggests. Pessimism and optimism are found in both collections. Camus believed that neither can ever abolish the other. In these essays "lucidity" calls for preserving a sense of balance between opposing attitudes.

Pessimism dominates *The Right Side and the Wrong Side*. A bitter observation, "death for us all, but his own death to each,"[3] unifies its essays. The work also reflects the profound sadness Camus felt in Prague where he had gone on holiday with Simone and a close friend, Yves Bourgeois, when the two ran off together. This caused the final break in the marriage. The moments of joy in the essays are outweighed by this experience, and the descriptions of illness. Following the completion of this book, Camus experienced his first bout of writer's block.[4]

Nuptials, however, is marked by a radical sensualism. Published in 1939, it highlights the wedding of man and earth as well as the rejection of sin and religion. In "The Winds of Djemila," Camus could write: "I think of flowers, smiles, the desire for women, and realize that my whole horror of death lies in my anxiety to live."[5]

Comparing the two works makes it clear that, for Camus, the pessimism of the earlier collection and the optimism of the latter affirm one another. But since optimism lacks justification, it can only exist in momentary eruptions and then, anticipating *The Myth of Sispyhus*, (*Le Mythe de Sisyphe*) again give way to pessimism. The tension between them is manifest. There is no reference to history or social situations. There is no possibility of progress or regression. We arbitrarily sway back and forth on the waves of opposing attitudes. We can only balance the one with the other as best as we can. "The Desert," which is the last essay of *Nuptials*, makes this clear:

It is on this moment of balance I must end: the strange moment when spirituality rejects ethics, when happiness springs from the absence of hope, when the mind finds its justification in the body. If it is true that every truth carries its bitterness within, it is also true that every denial contains a flourish of affirmations."[6]

The 1930s was a decade of powerful personalities: Churchill, Hitler, Mussolini, Roosevelt, and Stalin. It was culturally rich. It was dramatic. It was also a decade marked by counter revolution outside of the United States. The economic depression of 1929 spread over a European continent still reeling from World War I and its aftershocks. Republics that had arisen in the 1920s collapsed and the rest trembled. Fascism seemed to incarnate the future.

Dictators had already triumphed in Hungary in 1919, Poland in 1920, and the Baltic states. The fascists under Mussolini took power in Italy in 1921, more than a decade before the Nazis finally overthrew the newly-created German republic in 1933. Fascism blossomed in Austria and Finland. Its supporters in France clustered around the

Action Française, which posed a genuine threat to democracy, while a significant minority joined smaller and even more violent organizations. Fascism was an international phenomenon.

Everywhere, seemingly, opponents of fascism were divided and on the defensive. The political representatives of liberalism were identified with free-market capitalism and the interests of big business and did not have widespread popular support. The representatives of social democracy, which was embraced by the majority of workers, apparently lacked the will to fight in those states where fascism proved triumphant. Communism was embraced only by a radical minority of the European working class, and was dangerously sectarian. Isolated by the capitalist world, committed to world revolution, Lenin had already refused support for endangered "bourgeois" republican regimes in 1923. Stalin went even further in 1928 by identifying social democrats as "twin brothers" of the fascists. Nevertheless, this disciplined and ideologically militant movement at least seemed willing to fight the fascist enemy.

Camus ultimately made the same choice as many committed young anti fascists of his generation. In 1931 and 1932 Gustave Acault, his uncle, had introduced him to anarchist ideas for which the young nonconformist, who knew poverty so well, had a certain sympathy. Camus was never a sectarian, however, and he worked with Max-Pol Fouchet and the Young Socialists until their personal problems came between them. In 1934 a sense of political urgency gripped Camus. His mentor, Grenier, believed a small group of intelligent people could positively influence a weak if disciplined organization and suggested that his student join the Communist party in Algeria. Camus had his doubts from the beginning and he jotted into his notebook:

Grenier on Communism: "The whole question comes down to this: should one, for an ideal of justice, accept stupid ideas?" One can reply "yes," this is a fine thing to do. Or "no," it is honest to refuse.[7]

It is still not certain exactly when Camus joined the Communist party or even how long he remained a member. He later tried to downplay his association when purges were claiming the lives of millions in the Soviet Union. Most probably, however, Camus joined in 1934 or 1935 and remained a member until 1937.[8] There was a certain justification for his decision. A romantic aura still surrounded the communists in the 1930s. The U.S.S.R. was the homeland of the proletarian revolution. It was, in addition, the sole supporter of anti-imperialist struggles in colonized lands like Algeria. Its ideology reflected the concerns of the disempowered and disenfranchised whom Camus had known since childhood. It also seemed by late 1934 as if the communists would soon abandon their sectarian policy and work with other political parties.

★ ★ ★ ★ ★

Nineteen thirty-three had witnessed the formation of the Congress Against War and Fascism by pacifist writers like Romain Rolland and Henri Barbusse. By 1934 the need for unity seemed urgent as fascist rioting shook France. Socialists and Communists quickly responded with a pact pledging mutual support in the antifascist struggle. Their labor unions followed suit. A French Committee of anti fascist intellectuals was founded in 1934 and then, early in 1935, an international conference for the defense of culture took place. André Malraux and André Gide, who had recently joined the French Communist party, took part along with a host of other intellectual luminaries in this legendary event. Then, finally, on July 14, 1935, which commemorated the fall of the Bastille and marked the

André Malraux (left) and André Gide (seated) at the Writers Congress in Paris, 1936

French Revolution of 1789, antifascists from all the major parties came together and, in a demonstration of 500,000 in Paris, declared their intention to act together as a "Popular Front."

The coalition of parties known as the Popular Front scored a remarkable victory in the elections of 1936. Its tenure was brief, for the Popular Front was defeated in 1937 and only ruled again for a few months during 1938. However, its radical program of social and economic reforms laid the basis for the modern French welfare state. The Popular Front solidified the connection between liberalism and socialism and abolished the sectarianism of the 1920s. Its ideals inspired a new ethos of humanism and solidarity in any number of famous films and novels. Above all, however, the Popular Front gave hope to millions. A viable political strategy had, finally, been found to counter the spread of fascism.

Nowhere was this more important than in Spain. A republic had been created in 1931, replacing the Spanish monarchy. But it never won over the Catholic Church, the military, the aristocracy, or any of those other groups that had supported Fascist movements elsewhere in Europe. Under the leadership of General Francisco Franco, with promises of support from Hitler and Mussolini, the army staged a revolt in 1936. This action sparked a horrible civil war. Anarchists, communists, liberals, socialists, and Trotskyists responded by joining together to defend the republic in a Spanish version of the Popular Front.

Conflicts over economic policy, politics, and foreign policy quickly undermined the unity of the Popular Front in France. But these conflicts took an even more disastrous form in Spain. Anarchists and Trotskyists, who wished to carry forward a revolution while fighting the civil war, found themselves confronting a coalition of communists, social democrats, and bourgeois republicans

*Women supporters of the Popular Front movement march
in Paris in 1937*

who all opposed that idea for different reasons. This intractable division within the antifascist camp soon led to violence. With the communists in command, in 1937, the anarchist revolutionaries were massacred at the Battle of Barcelona. This sealed the Fascist victory. Nevertheless, the Spanish Civil War quickly became a symbol of revolutionary valor and antifascist resistance.

The Spanish events captured the imagination of Camus and others of his literary generation as well. Malraux published an underrated novel about the conflict, which was translated as *Man's Hope,* and Ernest Hemingway wrote *For Whom the Bell Tolls.* George Orwell initially made his literary reputation with *Homage to Catalonia* while Bertolt Brecht was inspired to write *The Rifles of Mother Carrar.* And there was more. Camus himself contributed to the ideological struggle in 1936 with his play *Revolt in the Asturias,* which identified with an uprising of anarchist Spanish miners in 1934. The play was written for the Workers Theater that Camus had founded in 1935. While he never gained a position of power within the Communist party, his cultural activity even more than his public speaking on significant issues made him one of its best known militants.[9]

Disillusionment with the communists ocurred soon enough, however, and its initial source was a seemingly innocuous invitation extended by Stalin to Pierre Laval in 1935. A minister in various conservative governments, and an arch reactionary, Laval would later lead the French Fascist government of Vichy after the French surrender to Germany in 1940. Stalin's invitation was clearly a friendly gesture to the French right, for Stalin now sought to embrace all possible allies in the antifascist cause. He was also willing to pay the price. While preparing for the Popular Front, Stalin insisted that communists sever their connection with the Algerian liberation struggle, to appease possible supporters with nationalist views.

Camus had initially opposed the inclusion of conservative antifascists in the Popular Front. He anticipated that they would attempt to change its economic policies even if he underestimated the difficulty of winning an election without them. He also stood in the forefront of those communists willing to work with Algerian nationalists. Camus was a prominent advocate of a bill initiated by Leon Blum, the socialist leader of the Popular Front, and Maurice Viollette, his minister of state, that would extend voting rights to 200,000 Muslims. But the prospect of its passage resulted in raucous demonstrations by French settlers and Stalin called upon communists to retract their support for the Blum-Viollette bill in order to pacify the French nationalists. Camus balked. Even worse, he broke the fundamental rule of the communists by taking his criticisms outside the confines of the organization. He was expelled in 1937 and, within the year, broke all ties with the communist movement.

Camus refused to renounce the democratic principles on which the Popular Front was based. But it was clear from the first that the Blum-Viollette bill would never reach the floor of the French parliament. It was also obvious that the new and less strident policy of the Communist party in Algeria was tactical and of little real importance anyway, given its meager size. As for the Laval visit, its prime purpose was to communicate Stalin's support for French rearmament in the face of a growing Nazi threat. This decision allowed the French communists to embrace patriotism by openly supporting rearmament.

Camus was never a nationalist. He was also an advocate of what the British prime minister, Neville Chamberlain, called "appeasement." This policy assumed that the territorial ambitions of fascist states, including Nazi Germany, were limited; its aim was to avoid war at all costs. Given the still-fresh memory of World War I at that time, the approach was not quite as foolish as it may now appear. Many brave and honorable people among all moderate and left-wing parties could join in the cry: "Never Again War!"

Appeasement began wearing thin, however, as the years passed and the scope of fascist domination increased. Japan conquered Manchuria; the world stood by. Italy invaded Abyssinia; its small and valiant army received no assistance. And then there was Hitler. He began rearming Germany in 1934, marched into the Rhineland in 1936, and annexed Austria in 1938. Each time Hitler threatened war and each time France and England backed down. Then, also in 1938, he called for severing the oil-rich Sudetenland from the Republic of Czechoslovakia and integrating it into Germany. This, he swore, would constitute his last territorial demand.

Edouard Daladier, Chamberlain, and Mussolini met with Hitler in Munich to decide the issue. Czechoslovakia played no role in the negotiations between its avowed enemies, Germany and Italy, and its allies, the Western democracies. England and France cynically agreed to Hitler's demand in exchange for a short-lived peace, and Camus supported the Munich Pact of 1938. That was perhaps understandable. Incomprehensible, however, was his continuing support for the policy of appeasement even after Hitler swallowed the remainder of Czechoslovakia and Winston Churchill replaced Chamberlain as prime minister. The Nazis attacked Poland in 1939, unleashing World War II. Camus tried to enlist out of simple solidarity with his countrymen, but was rejected for health reasons. Nevertheless, he continued to believe in negotiation.[10]

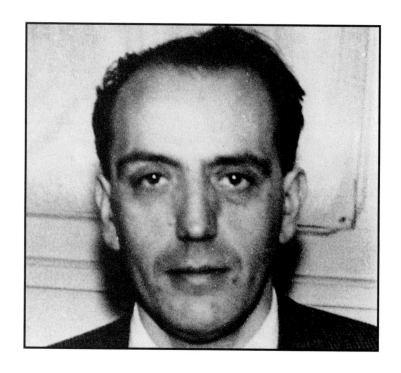

Pascal Pia

Camus was now earning his living as a journalist. A year earlier, in 1938, Pascal Pia had apppointed him to the staff of *Alger-Républicain*. Born in 1901, orphaned by the war, and poor, Pascal Pia entered bohemian circles at a young age. There he met the surrealist poet Louis Aragon who would later become an orthodox communist, as well as André Malraux with whom he became particularly close. Pia had been at the center of numerous scandals before becoming a newspaperman and deciding to run the new daily newspaper in Algiers. An anarchist of the spirit, a devotee of surrealism, Pia was one of those people who could remain in the background and work for the glory of his more talented friends. He did this for Malraux and Aragon. It would prove no different with Camus.[11]

*A group of loyalists defending Madrid in
the Spanish Civil War*

André Malraux

Pia taught Camus the journalistic craft. He took him along on his rounds of police stations, law courts, city council sessions, and the like. He supported Camus who began publishing literary reviews of "living works" by relatively unknown young writers such as Jean-Paul Sartre and Jean Giradoux. Under the tutelage of Pia, however, Camus primarily turned his attention to political matters. He wrote articles supporting the Spanish Republic, attacking attempts to roll back the reforms of the Popular Front, and criticizing the Treaty of Versailles for the burdens it placed on Germany in the aftermath of World War I. He also defended innocent victims of colonial injustice and police torture by noting that "when abject methods succeed in leading to the penal colony unhappy men whose life had already been only a series of miseries, then it represents for each of us a kind of personal injury that is impossible to accept."

Such words anticipate the themes of his more famous later writings. His gripping editorials exposed incompetence and called for European aid during the terrible Kabylian Famine of 1939. These articles created a sensation in Algiers and turned him into something of a celebrity.

Alger-Républicain was closed down during 1940 and, ironically, Camus found that his political interventions had made him unemployable.[12] So, when Pia found him a job as a reporter with *Paris-Soir* early in 1940, he decided to leave Algiers for the French capital. Upon arriving in France, however, he became profoundly depressed. He barely knew a soul. He also loathed working for this conservative mass market magazine owned by Jean Prouvoust, who would later join the Vichy government. The paper was preoccupied with crime, film stars, and scandal.

Camus saw the war as a product of human error and moral blindness.[13] But he was devastated nonetheless by the course of events. Adding to his depression was the gray gloom of the city, the cheap hotels, and the grinding poverty. Camus had just married Francine Faure, a pretty, physically delicate mathematician from a provincial middle-class family in Oran, Algeria. The separation from Francine was also depressing. Those dark times, however, inspired his notion of the absurd and introduced the world to three of its most dramatic representatives: Meursault, Sisyphus, and Caligula.

3

THE THREE ABSURDS

"THE THREE ABSURDS," CAMUS COULD NOTE IN HIS journal entry of February 21, 1941, "are now complete."[1] He was speaking about *The Stranger, The Myth of Sisyphus*, and *Caligula*. The three were written around the same time and stood together in his mind linked by a word: the absurd. It describes the meaninglessness of existence and was originally coined by the nineteenth-century Danish philosopher and religious thinker Søren Kierkegaard, who is also generally considered the founder of existentialism.

Of these three works, *The Stranger*, finished in 1940 and published in 1942, is the best known. Meursault, its main character, initially appears as someone uninterested in anything other than immediate physical sensations and honesty. He doesn't care about money or promotions and displays no feelings when his mother dies. He expresses no emotions at her funeral, other than discomfort in the heat, but he notices the most incidental objects like the screws in the coffin and the clothes people are wearing. The day of the funeral is a day like any other and, on the morrow, he goes swimming, where he meets a young girl whom he seduces. Meursault is polite, but remains emotionally distant. But he still takes Maria Cardona, who bears the name of Camus' grandmother, as his mistress.

One choice appears like the next and encounter follows encounter. Meursault goes again to the beach with his fiancée and his friend Raymond Sintés, whose last name is that of Camus' mother, along with his girl-friend. They chance upon a group of Arabs, who have a score to settle with Sintés; words are exchanged, the men scuffle, then they disperse. Blinded by the sun and looking for a spot of shade, however, Meursault returns and runs across one of the Arabs who flashes a knife. Meursault then fires a shot, and four more. The Arab lies dead.

The police arrest Meursault. He is then put on trial and condemned to death. But the reason for this extreme judgment has little to do with the murder. In Algeria, with the racist attitudes of the French colonial administrators, such an act would receive only a few years imprisonment. The real reason why the jury condemns Meursault stems from his refusal to explain his actions or lie about his inability to weep at his mother's funeral while being examined by the prosecutor. This "stranger" from himself and society subsequently waits for death. In prison, however, Meursault makes use of his memories and forgets the boredom that had defined his previous existence. The chaplain comes and is turned away.

Meursualt is passive, unreflective, and compulsive. He is a prototype of the "absurd man" who asks no questions and tells no lies. In his own way, however, he prizes honesty., and this makes it possible for him to change as the novel progresses. His refusal of communion and meta-physical hope occurs in the name of a new appreciation of physical life with its here and now. Meursault becomes his own person who, in this way, lives in the present and never simply resigns himself in the face of impending death. The closing pages of *The Stranger* with its beautiful evocation of individual experience, in fact, shows how the murderer has now learned to reconsider his existence through memory. Indeed, just before his execution, Meursault experiences "lucidity" regarding the richness of life and recognizes that he:

. . . felt ready to start life all over again. It was as if that great rush of anger had washed me clean, emptied me of hope and, gazing up at the dark sky spangled with its signs and stars, for the first time, the first, I laid my heart open to the benign indifference of the universe. To feel it so like myself, indeed, so brotherly, made me realize that I'd been happy and that I was happy still.[2]

Jean-Paul Sartre correctly called *The Stranger* a novel "about the absurd and against the absurd."[3] It offers a penetrating critique of the death penalty and "the world of a trial." But the possibility of judgment becomes tenuous. Thus, the novel threatens to plunge the reader into the very relativism its author claims to deny.

Camus saw his main character in a particular way. According to Camus, the story of Meursault is the "story of a man who, without any heroics, agrees to die for the truth."[4] The novel reveals an individualism to which Camus would be faithful for the rest of his life.[5]

The Myth of Sisyphus, completed in 1941 and published in 1943, seeks to illuminate a situation in which meaning has been withdrawn from the world. It offers a "lucid invitation to live and create in the very midst of the desert."[6] For this was how Camus saw the world. It is a "desert" in which religion has lost its foundation and science cannot offer an insight into the deep spiritual crisis experienced by the individuals of his generation.[7] Every absolute has been shattered and even philosophy must surrender any claim to "truth." Meaning is lost and a feeling of irremediable despair arises. Life becomes "absurd."

This idea of the absurd is usually associated with existentialism, which achieved popularity through the writings of Heidegger and Jaspers in the 1920s and Sartre in the 1930s and 1940s. Individual freedom is the basic concept embraced by all members of this philosophical trend. There is the need to develop some "authentic" mode of conduct for dealing with death or anxiety or guilt under circumstances in which an "absolute," such as God, is lacking. One ethical orientation is seemingly as legitimate as any other. While Camus attempts to distance himself from this tendency and assert his own perspective, the concerns in his writing are very similar to those of existentialism.

The absurd is a case in point. Camus views it as a particular encounter between an individual and the world in which the simple habit of living is called into question. This theme, which makes for a preoccupation with the "extreme" situation, is taken up by almost every existentialist. Camus is able to portray in particularly dramatic fashion, however, the way in which life can become a "habit" as well as "the absence of any profound reason for living, the insane character of that daily agitation and the uselessness of suffering."[8]

Camus also illuminates how suicide simultaneously becomes an expression of the absurd and a false response to this experience of the absurd. Suicide is an act of despair deriving from the need for meaning and the "muteness" of a meaningless world.[9] According to Camus, however, suicide capitulates to the absurd and therein lies its "inauthentic" quality. Thus, he can write:

In a way, suicide settles the absurd. It engulfs the absurd in the same death. But I know that in order to keep alive, the absurd cannot be settled. It escapes suicide to the extent that it is simultaneously awareness and rejection of death. . . . Consciousness and revolt, these rejections are the contrary of renunciation.[10]

Preserving the absurd without succumbing to it is incumbent upon the individual. But how? The "absurd man" can be a lover, an actor, or an adventurer. Essential

46

in each case, however, is the refusal of illusions and the willingness to use reason in coming to terms with one's situation. The individual must learn to live without the solace of religion or some prescribed purpose for history or existence. He or she, in short, must learn to "live *without appeal*."[11]

Sisyphus, the legendary figure of ancient Greece, exemplifies this imperative in the most dramatic way. Many are the stories surrounding this laborer of the underworld who was condemned by the gods to roll a huge boulder up a hill forever, watch it roll back down, and start again. Whether his punishment is for blasphemy, his desire to cheat death, or his love of other human beings at the expense of the gods matters little. He exemplifies the absurd hero. He accomplishes nothing; he receives no reward; he is alone. There is only the moment of consciousness, when he watches the rock roll back down the hill, and realizes that his refusal of all hope makes him superior to his fate.

Sisyphus, proletarian of the gods, powerless and rebellious, knows the whole extent of his wretched condition: it is what he thinks of during his descent. The lucidity that was to constitute his torture at the same time crowns his victory. . . . The struggle itself toward the heights is enough to fill a man's heart. One must imagine Sisyphus happy. [12]

Camus believed he was opposing all philosophical systems by stressing the uniqueness of individual experience and the role of happiness. His position claimed that the lack of a prescribed meaning creates the possibility of living life more fully. His criticisms of various existentialists, and their belief in generalistic theories and religious assumptions, are highly suspect. But his purpose in making those criticisms is not. Camus wished to carve out his own position at any price. He was confident in his artistic ability "to liberate my universe of its phantoms and to people it solely with flesh–and–blood truths whose presence I cannot deny."[13]

The Myth of Sisyphus appeared in France in 1943 in the midst of World War II when France was under the heel of the Nazis. It provided inspiration for the citizens of a defeated France and a symbol for the indomitable will of those who survived the concentration camps in Germany and the Soviet Union. This tale as told by Camus presents suicide as a form of resignation and, hence, as an illegitimate response to the absurdity of life. It also insists on the possibility of happiness without hope. *The Myth of Sisyphus*, for all these reasons, justifiably retains its salience precisely for those whose unlived possibilities most surely stretch before them: the young.

Camus was a young man in the 1930s. There was a marked difference between his peers and those who grew up before World War I. Young people all over the world in the 1930s considered democracy impotent, humanism worthless, and individualism decadent. Too many were drawn to the new movements led by dictators that demonized these ideals. Benito Mussolini, the founder of Italian fascism and chief of state, bragged about building a "New Rome"; Adolf Hitler, the German *führer* or leader, guaranteed an "Aryan" empire that would last a thousand years. Joseph Stalin, the dictator of the Soviet Union and leader of the world communist movement known as the Comintern, assured his dedicated followers that purges and artificial famines would lay the foundations for a communist paradise. Millions of lives were sacrificed and many millions more suffered war and deprivation for these utopian ends. When *Caligula* opened in 1945 in Paris, everyone understood the references in the play.

Camus was twenty-five when he finished the play in 1939, for his theater group in Algiers. He had initially become interested in the theater around the time he became active in politics. The *Theatre du Travail*, which he founded in 1935, provided him with a sense of community. After his break with the Communist party, however, Camus changed its name to the *Theatre de l'Equipe*. The troupe, which included Jeanne Sicard and Marguerite Dobrenn, remained the same and the program comprised a mixture of explicitly political, classical, and avant-garde drama.

Camus would remain fascinated by the theater. He wrote original plays from 1938 to 1949 and adapted various works of famous writers from 1953 to 1959. He acted in any number of parts during these earlier years and directed as well. André Malraux, who had become the minister of culture under General Charles de Gaulle, even offered Camus the leadership of the prestigious state-supported theater, the *Comedie Française*, in 1959. Intent on writing what would become his unfinished novel entitled *The First Man*, he declined.[14]

Caligula went through many drafts. Its main character was the emperor of Rome, legendary for his cruelty, who lived from A.D. 12 to 41. Camus had been introduced to the historical figure, Caligula, by the lectures of Jean Grenier. The play revolves around the arbitrary exercise of power by the infamous dictator. It shows how each of his whims becomes "necessary" for the realization of his utopian dream. It anticipates Camus' later criticisms of those who would sacrifice individuals in the name of abstract ideals. It exposes the price paid for divorcing means from ends. Above all, however, it portrays a figure who simply accepts the "absurd" and acts on its implications.

The play is set in ancient Rome after Caligula's ascension to the throne in A.D. 37. The young man is initially admired by his court; he is, says a scheming sychophant, "exactly the emperor we wanted: conscientious and inexperienced."[15] But, following the death of his beloved sister Drucilla, the young emperor is changed. Recognizing mortality, the fact that "men die and they are not happy,"[16] he is now filled with scorn for human frailty

Albert Camus as a young man

and "a desire for the impossible."[17] He experiences the "absurdity" of human existence and, as a consequence, becomes intent on making people live by the light of truth—as he perceives it.

He will use his power to carry all ideas to their logical conclusion. Caligula is a revolutionary, or better, an apocalyptic nihilist, who wants to change life itself. This finally leads to his assassination. Cherea, his former friend, who ultimately feels compelled to participate in the revolt against Caligula, puts the matter clearly:

> [Caligula is] putting his power at the service of a loftier, deadlier passion; and it imperils everything we hold most sacred. True, it's not the first time Rome has seen a man wielding unlimited power; but it's the first time he sets no limit to his use of it, and counts mankind, and the world we know, for nothing. That's what appalls me in Caligula; that's what I want to fight. To lose one's life is no great matter; when the time comes I'll have the courage to lose mine. But what's intolerable is to see one's life being drained of meaning, to be told there's no reason for existing. A man can't live without some reason for living.[18]

Totalitarianism shows its face in the figure of Caligula and Camus indicates why he must engage himself against it. He is disgusted by a situation in which a person can be killed at whim and wherein "the most preposterous fancy may at any moment become a reality." He is repulsed by the arrogance of those who, even with respect to religion, cannot "deny something without feeling called on to besmirch it, or deprive others of the right of believing in it."[19] Such values and behavior, according to Camus, call forth revolt by any decent person. And not just against Caligula or Hitler, but, in principle, against any dictator.

Maria Casarès

4

WORLD WAR

WORLD WAR II CHANGED THE YOUNG WRITER. OR IT shifted his focus. He was no longer preoccupied with the plight of the individual in a meaningless world. He became concerned with solidarity and the ethics of resistance. From September 1939 to March 1940, the war between Germany and France was at a stalemate. In April of 1940, however, the German armies crossed the border and, after a brief period of fighting, entered Paris in June. Camus experienced something new during this time in which each person, employing a phrase from the play, *State of Siege*, "was in the same boat."

In the ensuing war years and the immediate postwar years Camus became established as a public figure and grew close to Jean-Paul Sartre and Simone de Beauvoir. He came to know Arthur Koestler and Malraux, the poet Michel Leiris, and the brilliant political essayist Raymond Aron. He also fell in love with Maria Casarès, the actress, now best remembered for her minor part in the film *Children of Paradise* (*Les Enfants de Paradis*). Daughter of the former Spanish prime minister Casarès Quiroga, she had

Simone de Beauvoir

worked as a volunteer nurse during the Spanish Civil War while hardly a teenager. She would star in a number of Camus' plays and often break off their stormy affair over his stubborn refusal to leave Francine. Nevertheless, whether as a lover or a friend, Maria Casarès remained his constant campanion.[1]

Hers was perhaps the most emotionally charged of the intense friendships forged by Camus in the cafés of St. Germain des Prés, underground cultural events, parties at people's homes, and countless meetings. Novels like *The Mandarins* (*Les Mandarins*) by de Beauvoir, a *roman á clef* in which Camus is featured as a promiment character, would beautifully describe the cultural and political climate as well as how most of these friendships soured after the war. But the bitterness of defeat initially generated a new sense of solidarity, perhaps more intense than that of the Popular Front if just as short-lived, and a hope for the postwar renewal of France from which the legend of the "resistance" was born. Indeed, "out of the Resistance, directly or indirectly, came nearly every advanced social movement or current of ideas that stirred French opinion from the end of the war until the mid-1950s."[2]

Defeat produced a remarkable response. General Charles de Gaulle fled to London and, with the help of his supporters, created an antifascist government in exile. Simultaneously, seemingly everywhere in France, resistance groups sprang into existence. Communists stood in the forefront; their discipline, their hierarchical form of organization, and their commitment to fighting the Nazis drew them many new members. Even people who were previously nonpolitical found themselves drawn into some form of opposition against Hitler and his puppet ruler of Nazi-occupied France, Marshal Pétain. A solidarity emerged among the opponents of the Nazis, for anyone in the Resistance risked capture, and

Soldiers of the German conquering army in Paris

imprisonment or deportation by the Nazis no matter how minor their role.

Camus was relatively isolated in the early days folowing the French defeat. After *Paris-Soir* laid him off in order to cut costs in December of 1940, he returned to North Africa. The next two years were spent with Francine living a rather frugal existence in Oran, which was the second largest city in French Algeria. She took a position as a substitute teacher in an elementary school while Camus worked as an editorial adviser for *Editions Charlot.* He also coached a soccer team, and taught "French studies" part-time at two schools set up exclusively for

Jews by the collaborationist Vichy government ruling Algeria.

Camus was too well known to serve a useful role in the Algerian resistance effort. He helped arrange escapes for those who wished to leave Vichy-controlled Algeria for Morocco or elsewhere. But, for all that, Camus' existence was relatively uneventful. Then, in August of 1942, an attack of tuberculosis led him to convalesce at a sanatorium in Le Panelier, about thirty-five miles south of Lyons, in mainland France, where he began work on *The Plague* (*La Peste*).

There he was caught unaware and separated from his wife by the allied landing in North Africa, the first stage in the invasion of Italy, in November of 1942. Much time passed before he joined the Resistance toward the end of 1943. His hesitation is somewhat difficult to explain since a National Council of the Resistance (CNR) had already been organized and an antifascist network had existed for some time in the neighboring town of Saint-Etienne while Jews were regularly being smuggled out of France from nearby Cambon-sur-Lignon.

Camus was never a major leader of the Resistance, even if he cultivated that image after the war.[3] He had entered too late. Once he finally joined, however, he made an exceptional contribution as an anonymous writer and editor of the legendary underground paper *Combat*.[4] It advocated a "collectivized economy with political freedom." The slogan of its editor was "justice and liberty."[5]

Combat sent Camus back to Paris during 1943 where he lived first in a hotel and then in the flat of Andre Gide that Gallimard, his new publisher, had secured for him along with a modest monthly stipend. Camus would not meet Gide until 1945, but his apartment became a center of intellectual life for the Resistance. Camus quickly made friends with important figures of the Resistance like Father Bruckberger, who would later greet de Gaulle at the Notre Dame cathedral on his triumphant entry into Paris following the liberation; the communist poet,

André Gide, French author and Nobel prize winner

François Pongé, who would become an intimate friend; and another poet, René Leynaud, chief of the Paris sector of the *Comité Nationale de la Resistance* (CNR), whom the Gestapo would execute in 1944.

Camus admired the man enormously for his modesty and his bravery. The now famous *Letters to a German Friend* (*Lettres á un Ami Allemand*) were dedicated to his memory.[6] The first of these letters was published in 1943, and the next three in 1944, in *Combat*. They became known throughout France. Written to justify taking up arms against the Nazis by the Resistance, the arguments are emotional rather than reasoned. They evoke stark images of how a defeated population was forced to live "with humiliations and silences, with prison sentences, with executions at dawn, with desertions and separations, with daily pangs of hunger, with emaciated children, and, above all, with humiliation of our human dignity."[7]

★ ★ ★ ★ ★

The *Letters to a German Friend* also emphasize the moral cost to the victim of using violence to counter violence. Traces of his former pacifism surface once again as Camus wonders "if we had the right to kill men, if we were allowed to add to the frightful misery of this world." Within the framework of propaganda, these letters meditate on the motivations for engagement and reflect the change a generation underwent. Camus notes how:

We had to make a long detour, and we are far behind. It is a detour that regard for truth imposes on intelligence, that regard for friendship imposes on the heart. It is a detour that safeguarded justice and put truth on the side of those who questioned themselves. And, without a doubt, we paid very dearly for it.[8]

Two traditions are shown in conflict: fascism and humanism, irrationalism and enlightenment, force and what the French call *civilisation*. The ideological reasons for the war become clear in these letters along with an understanding of what drove young men and women into the Resistance. They evidence the wearying effect of clandestine meetings, the constant threat of arrest, and the death of so many friends. The letters also make plain the concern with issues of solidarity and conscience, which would become so pronounced in the next phase of his literary career.

5

THE PLAGUE

THE MISUNDERSTANDING (LE MALENTENDU), WHICH
was also written during the war in 1943, marks the
change undergone by Camus. The drama portrays the
world of the occupation. Its unrelieved gloom and
claustrophobic quality probably makes it easier to read
than to see.[1] Perhaps this helps explain its sharply critical
reception when it was first performed in 1944, under the
occupation, with Maria Casarès in the lead.[2] The plot is
simple and somewhat contrived. Martha and her mother
own a little hotel in a remote valley. They are poor and
support themselves by poisoning and robbing any rich
travelers who happen upon their establishment. One such
visitor is Jan, the long lost son. He has returned from far
away with money for his family. But he wishes to be
recognized without giving his name. Maria, his wife, begs
Jan to act sensibly and present himself to his family. He
remains adamant, however, and sends his wife away,
fearing she will betray his identity.

His decision is perhaps understandable as a whim.
With the heightening of the dramatic tension, however, it

makes less sense why Jan should keep his secret. His mother and sister harbor some momentary hesitations about committing yet another murder. But the doubts vanish in the face of habit. Using the storyline of *Oedipus the King* by Sophocles, which deals with a son who unwittingly sleeps with his mother and kills his father, the tragedy of Camus reaches a climax with the murder of the son by his mother and sister.

After learning the identity of the victim, the mother commits suicide, while the daughter feels her hopes for a better future destroyed. Maria, for her part, is simply stunned by the news of her husband's death. Martha has no sympathy for her sister-in-law and, following a tense confrontation, Maria cries out for help. But the old manservant, silent until then, answers: "No." With that the curtain falls.

The stilted language and the gothic plot undermine this "attempt to create a modern tragedy."[3] Neither critical reflection nor identification with the one-dimensional characters is made easy: Jan is stubborn. Maria is helpless and weak. The mother is worn down by her existence; she wants this murder to be the last one; and there is a pathetic quality to her suicide following the realization that she has murdered her son. Martha may elicit some sympathy as she so desparately wishes to leave her depressing valley for a country by the sea. But she is both selfish and self-pitying; indeed, even had she known the visitor was her brother, "it would have made no difference."[4]

Tyranny infuses everyday life with suspicion and sets people against one another. People turn inward and the sense of community dissolves as the reality sets in that "it's easier to kill what one doesn't know."[5] And this highlights the importance of language, which alone makes it possible to establish connections with others. "Silence is fatal," the mother tells her daughter. "But speaking is as dangerous; for the little that [Jan] said, only hurried the tragic end."[6]

For Camus, it is now a matter of finding the "appropriate word" in order to identify oneself and intervene in the world. But, of course, this is precisely what Jan refuses to do. In keeping silent, he cuts himself off from others and expects intuition to do the work of reason. That is impossible. Only with language is it possible to deal with a "meaningless" existence and genuinely identify with the sufferings inflicted on the weakest members of society.

★ ★ ★ ★ ★

The Plague is a major novel of World War II. Ironically, however, it was conceived before the war and written while Camus was convalescing in Central France where there was no fighting. There he felt the war as an absence,[7] which is why he deals neither with battles nor the singular acts of wartime heroism, but the everyday life of a populace under siege.

The Plague crystallized the experience of a generation sick of war, guilty about its early defeat, and suspicious about the future. Indeed, it "represents the transition from an attiude of solitary revolt to the recognition of a community whose struggles must be shared. If there is an evolution from *The Stranger* to *The Plague*, it is in the direction of solidarity and participation.[8] It also provides perhaps the best understanding of Camus' political worldview. It contains his critique of Christianity, his refusal to love a god who lets the innocent die and who demands unconditional acceptance of the human condition.

This novel reflects the humanistic values of the Popular Front and, like so many other works from the 1930s and 1940s, it has no protagonist. Its characters engage in political action almost as a last resort and long for a return to private life. There are no grand words and no grand gestures. There is in the novel's words "no question of heroism in all of this. It's a matter of common decency. That's an idea which may make some people smile, but the only means of fighting the Plague is— common decency."[9]

A "chronicle" begins with rats dying in the town of Oran and leaving the Plague as their legacy. People start becoming incurably ill and the authorities, after first attempting to downplay these developments, cling to habit and refuse to accept the evidence of an epidemic. Thus, ultimately, they find themselves without any plan for dealing with the emergency.

At this point Tarrou, who keeps a diary of the Plague, unites a motley group of individuals with very different world views into a "sanitation corps" committed to fight the Plague. Rieux is a doctor who can no longer heal; Grand is a clerk, who wishes to write a novel, but cannot get beyond the first sentence; Rambert is a journalist torn between love for his mistress, whom he wishes to join in another city, and the growing sense of solidarity with the inhabitants of Oran; Paneloux is a priest who, from the pulpit, calls the Plague a punishment from God and then witnesses the death of an innocent child; and finally there is Tarrou, a humanist and an opponent of the death penalty.

Which of the characters is most "like" the author is irrelevant. Rieux exemplifies the militant who, like Camus, doesn't subscribe to any particular political creed and quietly engages in the unheralded day to day battle with tyranny; he is "the modern Sisyphus."[10] Tarrou, like Camus, opposes capital punishment and seeks inner peace through his *morale de compréhension*. Joseph Grand, who could never complete his perfect work of art and reflects the writer's block often experienced by Camus himself, evidences his dignity by engaging in the humble task of keeping careful statistics of the Plague. Rambert is separated from his lover, just as Camus was separated from Francine, and in staying to fight the Plague makes perhaps the ulitimate personal sacrifice in the name of solidarity.[11] For all his Catholic dogmatism, which Camus experienced while again convalescing at a Dominican monastery in 1943, Father Paneloux reflects the courage of his convictions. Each of these characters exhibits something with which Camus identifies, and in the solidarity they exhibit as well as the sacrifices they make, he finds "more things in men to admire than to despise."

The novel offers no certainty, however, that the struggle against the epidemic was of any use. Resistance does not defeat the Plague, but only bears witness against it. the Plague seems to subside on its own and Rieux, who ultimately emerges as the narrator of the novel, ruefully acknowledges to himself

what those jubilant crowds did not know but could have learned from books: that the plague bacillus never dies or disappears for good . . . and that perhaps the day would come when, for the bane and enlightening of men, it would rouse up its rats again and send them forth to die in a happy city.[12]

★ ★ ★ ★ ★

Roland Barthes, the great literary critic, called *The Plague* a "refusal of history." For this novel of World War II clearly meant "the Plague" to stand for the Nazi rulers of France. Numerous critics have noted that the real nature of fascism is ignored and the battle against an inhuman plague oversimplifies the matter of commitment. Violence carried out against a human enemy is very different from the tactics undertaken in fighting the Plague.

This critique attacks Camus for not having written the "realist" work these critics wanted to read.[13] *The Plague* does not pretend to describe the horrors of totalitarianism. The province of a symbolic tale is the moral conflicts experienced by individuals. The criticism of Barthes and others like Sartre ignores the manner in which the novel actually offers an understanding of the Resistance by a Resistance member.

*The swastika, the Nazi emblem, was a common
sight in Nazi-occupied Paris.*

Participants in the Resistance saw themselves engaged in the battle against absolute evil; men and women of very different creeds united in a common project.[14] Camus glorifies them and perhaps *The Plague* helped foster the "myth" of the Resistance. It offers "an idealised reconstruction of the movement such as Camus and others would have liked it to have been: the fight of a virtuous and oppressed minority against an anonymous and depersonalized aggressor."[15] But the novel also contests the carefully cultivated postwar image of the vast majority of the French as antifascist. *The Plague* depicts the majority as apathetic and falling back into a life of habit as the Plague runs its course.

Disease as the symbol of evil has a long history. Symbolically identifying totalitarianism with a plague obscures the character of a particular political system. Evil has no name, no race, no sex, and no nationality. It is part of the human condition. For this reason, however, Camus could refuse to identify any one form of evil "in order better to strike at them all. . . . *The Plague* can apply to any resistance against tyranny."[16]

Germaine Brée termed *The Plague* a "cautionary tale."[17] The doctors are warned about taking the necessary precautions in treating the victims lest they themselves become carriers of the disease.[18] In the words of Tarrou, what Camus would consider the basic issue of the age becomes defined:

As time went on I merely learned that even those who were better than the rest could not keep themselves nowadays from killing or letting others kill, because such is the logic by which they live; and that we can't stir a finger in this world without the risk of bringing death to somebody.[19]

There is not a single Communist among the prominent figures in the novel. Rieux, Tarrou, Grand, and Rambert are all liberal humanists; Paneloux is a Catholic. Communists played a prominent role in the French resistance. Camus' decision to omit them was thus surely purposeful.

Neither Victims Nor Executioners, which appeared in 1946, was composed of Camus' last writings for *Combat*. The collection emphasized the sanctity of the individual and explicitly criticized not only fascism, but Stalinism for its perverse belief that a utopian future justifies the use of systematic murder in the present. These themes were also prominent in *Caligula*. In *The Plague*, respect for the individual becomes the foundation for solidarity among people. Camus proposes the more modest attempt to "correct existence" and forge a new "rule of conduct in secular life."[20] Such was the message of *The Plague* when it appeared in 1947.

6

POSTWAR PARIS

CAMUS WAS ALREADY A BUDDING STAR EVEN BEFORE
the publication of *The Plague*. *The Stranger* and *The Myth
of Sisyphus* had gained him a following, and he was
admired as the editor of *Combat*. On his visit to the
United States and South America, which he described in
his *American Journals*, he was hailed as the most talented of
the new French writers.[1] He had also become a father
and head of a household as his wife, Francine, gave birth
to twins—Jean and Catherine—in 1945. With the publication of *The Plague*, moreover, Camus conquered poverty. The novel, which soon sold over one hundred
thousand copies and was quickly translated into many
languages,[2] turned him into an international celebrity. His
lifestyle changed. He now made the little city of
Lourmarin his summer home, kept an apartment on Saint
Germain des Prés, and spent the winters in Oran. Camus
started wearing expensive suits, drove a black Citröen, and
let himself be seen with beautiful women by reporters
who followed his movements around the "left bank" of
Paris.

Francine Camus holding the twins,
Jean and Catherine Camus

Camus enjoyed his fame. But he didn't shirk the new public responsibilities that came with it. The Popular Front of the past was dead. A new version of this progressive coalition never came to fruition. Three interconnected issues had led to its dissolution in the aftermath of World War II: the problem of the collaborators, the Communist party, and the national liberation movement in Algeria. Each would have a profound impact on the career of Albert Camus.

Writing in *Combat* about the collaborators—those French citizens who had supported the Vichy government and its policies—he advocated a policy of "justice without mercy" as the prelude to a radical socialist transformation of French society. A purge of Fascists seemed necessary at both the highest and lowest levels of society. A new judicial system was not yet operating in the immediate aftermath of the liberation, however, and those suspected of treason were often simply taken into custody, summarily punished, or even executed. More than 10,000 people are believed to have died in this purge. Camus grew increasingly disgusted with the executions. Ultimately he agreed publicly with the the great Catholic novelist, Nobel prize winner, and member of the resistance, François Mauriac.[3] Earlier Mauriac had criticized Camus' disregard for legal issues and his overzealous attitude. Camus had learned his lesson. He would never again speak in favor of the death penalty and he would remain staunch in his defense of civil liberties.

A new, democratic Fourth Republic was established in 1946 following the defeat of the Nazis and the collapse of the Vichy government. But hopes for a socialist transformation of French society withered. Charles de Gaulle became the first president of the Fourth Republic, and the communists embraced a new sectarian line. Conservatives and remnants of the old

*François Mauriac, French author, resistance member,
and winner of the Nobel prize*

right now gathered around de Gaulle. Camus annoyed them by calling for an international boycott of Spain, which was still under the fascist yoke of Generalissimo Francisco Franco. In 1948 he helped found the *Groupe de Liaison Internationale*, which sought to give both moral and financial aid to political refugees regardless of their ideology. His opposition to the death penalty and commitment to the politically persecuted, however, also put him directly at odds with the French communists who were defending the bloody purges throughout Eastern Europe as well as, once again, in Russia itself.

Understanding postwar Europe is possible only by recognizing the respect enjoyed by the Communist party, particularly in those western countries previously controlled by the Nazis. The Soviet Union had supported the Spanish republican loyalists against Franco and opposed the "appeasement" of Hitler when he invaded Czechoslovakia in 1938. The pact between Stalin and the German dictator, which had resulted in the dismemberment of Poland in 1939, was now interpreted as a defensive action caused by the vacillation of the democracies.

The Soviet Union gained much sympathy for its enormous losses during the war; its citizens symbolized antifascist heroism in the great battle of 1943 for the city of Stalingrad, which was besieged and starved by Nazi troops for nearly two years, but never surrendered. The failed siege of Stalingrad was the turning point of the war and this only increased the prestige of the communists. They also played a valiant role in the European resistance movements, and communist-led organizations commanded the loyalty of a significant number of workers in France and Italy, and elsewhere after World War II. The Soviet Union was still considered the natural ally of national liberation movements in the Third World and the primary opponent of Western imperialism. The future of communism

Albert Camus in 1951

appeared bright and the "inevitability" of world revolution seemed assured.

Exiles and victims obviously knew about the murderous purges of opponents, the concentration camps, the censorship, the constant lying of the Stalinist regime. But the full horror of the "dictatorship of the proletariat," or its sacrifice of millions for the dreams of an egalitarian society was not fully grasped. Arthur Koestler, with whom Camus enjoyed a tempestuous friendship, vividly crystallized this reality in *Darkness at Noon*.

The novel, which first appeared in 1940, described a former Bolshevik official coming to terms with his beliefs and previous actions on behalf of the party while facing death in a Stalinist prison. It created a sensation and was instantly condemned by various communists and intellectual sympathizers including, most notably, Maurice Merleau-Ponty. Best known for his work on existential phenomenology, Merleau-Ponty was an early friend of Jean-Paul Sartre who would later sharply criticize his political theory in *Adventures of the Dialectic*. At the time, however, he stood closer to the Communist party than most of its non-aligned supporters.

His rejoinder to Koestler, *Humanism and Terror*, justified the authoritarian brutality of Stalinism as a "historical necessity" on the march to a communist utopia. Even if the criticisms made by Koestler were true, Merleau-Ponty thought it necessary to oppose them since they weakened the Soviet Union and strengthened its Western "imperialist" adversaries in a "Cold War" that could end in nuclear catastrophe.

Camus was caught in the middle. He did not support the Western countries' exploitation of colonies, ranging from Algeria to Vietnam, nor the brutal policies of the Soviet Union in Eastern Europe. Just after the war, Camus had witnessed the bloody repression of the first

*A café in St. Germain des Prés, the haunt of
the artists, writers, and intellectuals associated with
existentialism in the postwar period*

Muslim uprising in Algeria against French imperialist rule. His ensuing critical essays were so precise and clear in their demands for Algeria that he was offered a government position. Camus refused, of course, especially since the army and various conservative groups both in France and in Algeria adamantly opposed liquidating the French empire. Governmental cabinet after cabinet was paralyzed by the intransigence of right-wing members. The Socialist party, weakened by the Algerian question, was unable to overcome mounting internal political battles. Thus, while the Resistance was fragmenting into communist and Gaullist factions, Camus increasingly found himself supporting a liberal socialism whose base of support was disintegrating.

Camus refused to make a dogmatic choice between the two sides. His concern about the authoritarian cliques surrounding General de Gaulle caused tensions between himself and André Malraux, who held a government position. The communists, for their part, deplored his unwavering commitment to civil rights and republican principles. Camus sought a Scandinavian form of democratic socialism. But he had never really articulated a political theory or his fundamental criticisms of the communist worldview and its philosophical foundations. He began the undertaking with two plays that indicate a connection between critical conviction and political engagement, *State of Siege* (1948) and *The Just Assassins* (1949).

State of Siege (*État de Siège*) was conceived as a medieval morality play and a testament to the antifascist struggle in Spain.[4] The action begins with a bad omen, a comet passing over the walled city of Cadiz. The authorities intent on maintaining the routine of everyday life, insist that this did not occur and should not be discussed by the inhabitants of the town. Preparations are not undertaken and when the Plague—who appears as a man in uniform—finally enters, he easily assumes control of the city with the help of a cynical nihilist, Nada (Spanish for nothing), who does not care what government is in power.

The Plague, like all dictators, equates the right to power with the fact of power. He introduces a number of arbitrary and noxious decrees that contradict their allegedly beneficial aims. For the sake of protecting them against infection, all citizens are required to keep a pad soaked with vinegar in their mouth at all times and, for purposes of preventing contagion, people are assumed guilty of having the sickness until proven innocent. The sickness isolates people in the community and the authorities impose drastic measures to end, including executions. Diego is led to revolt. The Plague responds with threats against the hero's lover, Victoria. Diego offers to exchange his life for hers. The Plague refuses, but makes a counteroffer: he is willing to end the sickness in exchange for both their lives. Diego is unwilling to compromise the innocent, in this case, Victoria. The reign of the Plague is brought to an end by the solidarity of common people, though his reappearance remains still possible. But the moral point is that Diego can only choose for himself. Coherence must exist between ends and means.

The Just Assassins (*Les Justes*) more dramatically sets the limits on revolt. Set in prerevolutionary Russia, it revolves around a plot by a group of anarchists to assassinate a Grand Duke. Its strong characters with differing temperaments and ethical views are all dedicated revolutionaries. Kaliayev goes on his mission and is ready to throw the bomb when he realizes the Archduke's wife and innocent children would die in the explosion as well. He refuses to act, returns to the group, where a discussion of his decision takes place and Dora, one of Camus' best female characters, stresses that the genuine revolutionary never forgets the empathy with suffering that inspired his actions in the first place. Kaliayev then tries again and succeeds in killing the Grand Duke. He is captured and sentenced to be hanged, but refuses to betray his comrades in exchange for his life. Two basic moral positions of Camus in this way become clear: the creation of a just society in the future cannot rest on the unjust sacrifice of innocent individuals in the present; and only when when a life is exchanged for a life—and even then the actual political value of the action remains uncertain—is it possible to speak about a moral basis for murder.

None of these ethical themes is spelled out with philosophical rigor. Camus only began thinking systematically about the question of murder in the aftermath of the Koestler affair. Already while working on *The Myth of Sisyphus*, however, Camus had begun collecting notes for a volume concerning the legitimacy of murder. Its completion would prove difficult for him. He again suffered from writer's block. He questioned his ability to produce a treatise with the requisite philosophical, political, and literary depth. Perhaps Camus had a presentiment of what would result from its publication. His new work would indeed create a windstorm of controversy, isolate him politically, and cause the breakup of his friendship with Jean-Paul Sartre. *The Rebel* would become his first, and last, work of political theory.

THE REBEL

THE REBEL, WHICH APPEARED IN 1951, COMPLETED the second cycle of Camus' writings. It proposes a positive political response to an absurd existence and simultaneously expresses a revulsion against an age in which mass murder was an acceptable political option. Both feelings are encompassed in the title, *L'Homme Révolté*, which has a double meaning in French: the rebel and the revolted man.

The work is divided into three parts: revolutionary transformation, artistic rebellion, and political ethics based on "Mediterranean thinking." In the first section on politics, the idea of radical social change advocated by Marx and Lenin assumes that individuals are expendable. This trend was deepened by cultural modernism, which is discussed in the second part. Its principal exponents, beginning with the Marquis de Sade, were intent on abolishing all values and customs of the past. Revolution was turned into an undertaking that has no limits on action. The third section of *The Rebel* is an attempt to reinstate the ethical limits on action, to emphasize a

"Mediterranean" moderation, and to reassert the connection between rebellion and respect for human life and dignity.

The Rebel and *The Myth of Sisyphus* are coherently related. We live in an "absurd" universe. Suicide is an inadequate response to it. But so is rebellion when it assumes that "everything is possible and nothing has any importance."[1] Suicide is illegitmate insofar as it denies the sanctity of life. The killing of another person cannot prove moral unless, in keeping with *The Just Assassins*, the murderer is himself or herself prepared to die as well. Herein lies the "limit" to rebellion and the meaning behind the belief of Camus that "murder and suicide are the same thing: one must either accept or reject them both."

Rebellion, for Camus, is a product of human nature. It is the practical expression of outrage at injustice, be it by a slave or anyone else who has experienced the transgression of an established limit by a master. The exploited or oppressed person wants to be treated as a person with basic rights and dignity. The legitimate goal of countering exploitation is often used, however, to justify tactics directly at odds with it.[2] All tactics then assume legitimacy including those involving the murder of any who stand in the way of constructing a just world. The end is seen as justifying the means; claims about the need for progress are used to justify acts of murder by the state. Therein, according to Camus, lies the "pathology" of modern totalitarianism.

The Rebel must assume that life has an intrinsic worth, otherwise why would he or she have contested injustice in the first place? But, if this is the case, then commitment to the vision of a perfect world must be tempered by compassion. The genuine rebel, for this reason, continually strives to remember his or her motivation when faced with the temptation of unethical action against others. The communist followers of Marx forgot this along with those Nazis who perverted the thought of Nietzsche.

Even as a young man, Camus would maintain that

Politics are made for men, and not men for politics. We do not want to live on fables. In the world of violence and death around us, there is no place for hope. But perhaps there is room for civilization, for real civilization, which puts truth before fables and life before dreams. And this civilization has nothing to do with hope. In it, man lives on his truths.[3]

The Rebel legitimately insists on the connection between means and ends. Its spirit anticipates the nonviolent and ideologically liberal mass movements of 1989, which brought about the fall of communism. It is concerned with mitigating injustice and fostering the "moderation" of reformist politics. It emphasizes discussion as well as a sense of the concrete experiences of injustice that fuel rebellion; "I did not learn rebellion in Marx," Camus could write, "but in misery." The book combines elements of liberalism, socialism, and even anarchism.[4]

But, if *The Rebel* was conceived as a philosophical treatise and a work of political theory, there is some question as to whether it fully succeeds as either. Camus said nothing new about totalitarianism or, for that matter, the importance of civil liberties and republican values. It is unclear how moderation, a concept already emphasized by Aristotle, can inspire a new form of rebellion. Enough Nazis and communists, moreover, joined their movements in order to eradicate what they saw as injustice and were also quite willing to die in exchange for the death of their opponents in brawls and street battles.

Communist hacks blasted the book unmercifully when it appeared and, Conservatives and Catholics applauded Camus for showing how revolutions only

Jean-Paul Sartre

produce new hangmen.[5] Even liberal critics who supported his attack on utopianism and his identification with democratic values were skeptical about some of his philosophical claims such as the absolute value of rebellion. Thus, there were already doubts about *The Rebel* before Camus engaged in his bitter debate with Jean-Paul Sartre, the dominant figure of modern French existentialism.

Camus and Sartre became friends during the Nazi occupation. Both grew famous early in life. Sartre was older. Born in 1905 of an upper middle-class family in Alsace and a cousin of the great humanist Albert Schweitzer, he had studied philosophy at the famous *Ecole Normale Supérieure*. Sartre was short, ugly, talkative, and a man of the city. He despised religion, liberalism, and everything connected with the bourgeoisie. He was, physically and psychologically, almost the mirror opposite of Camus. But, whatever the differences between them, their work dealt with similar themes: the individual, the absurd, freedom, and responsibility. Both were antifascists. They associated with the same circle of people and, following the liberation, contributed to the intellectual glitter of the Parisian "left bank."

Much has been written about the relations between these two leading intellectuals of their generation. But Simone de Beauvoir, author of the legendary work of feminism *The Second Sex* (La Deuxième Sexe) and the lifelong companion of Sartre, noted in her extraordinary autobiography that "if this friendship exploded so violently, it was becuase for a long time not much of it had remained."[6] She tells the story of how, in 1946, Camus came to a party and encountered Merleau-Ponty whom he sharply criticized for his review of Koestler's "The Yogi and the Commissar" and his justification of the terrible Moscow purge trials of the 1930s. Sartre intervened on the side of Merleau-Ponty, and Camus left in a huff. Sartre caught up with him in the street, and begged him to return, but Camus refused. This was the beginning of their estrangement.

Their admirers have created a competition between Camus and Sartre, and the two men had indeed become rivals by 1952. They competed for a similar audience, they chose different political paths, and each became more suspicious about the ambitions of the other. Camus believed his friend was creating an uncritical "mystique" of the working class, while Sartre saw Camus' concern with democracy and limited revolt being used to justify Western imperialism. Both were right in part. While Sartre never recognized any reactionary prejudices on the part of the working class or the oppressed, Camus increasingly found himself cast into the despised role of a reactionary anticommunist.

The burgeoning mistrust broke into the open with a review of *The Rebel* by François Jeanson in the legendary journal *Les Temps Modernes*, founded and edited by Sartre. Camus had apparently asked his colleague to arrange a review, without suggesting any reviewer in particular, and Jeanson had volunteered. The result was not what Camus, or Sartre himself for that matter, had expected. Rather than treating *The Rebel* tactfully, as he had originally implied he would, Jeanson attacked Camus for his superficial philosophical interpretations of Hegel and Marx as well as for his rejection of revolution without offering any positive or practical content for his vision of rebellion. Camus was furious. Suspecting that Jeanson was merely acting as the front-man for Sartre, he wrote a response to *Monsieur l'editeur*. Camus dismissed Jeanson, implying he was "unworthy" of reviewing his book, and also attacked Sartre and the rest of the editorial board of *Les Temps Modernes*. He called them bourgeois intellectuals and Stalinists unwilling to condemn the concentration camp universe in the Soviet Union.

Sartre responded to Camus in a biting polemic.[7] He charged Camus with exchanging his earlier non-conformism and commitment to revolt for a fashionable anticommunism. He presented Camus' condemnation of the excesses of both sides in the Cold War as a rejection of genuine political "engagement" and an inability to choose between the imperialists and their victims. There was also a personal attack, and Sartre knew where to push the buttons. He castigated Camus for his arrogant treatment of Jeanson, his sensitivity to criticism, his self-professed weariness with politics, and his moral posturing. Coming from someone who presumably knew Camus well, this probably carried greater weight with the public than the political arguments.

Each exaggerated the position of the other.[8] Sartre knew that Camus was not some reactionary anti-communist.[9] For his part, Camus knew that Sartre had steadfastly refused to join the Communist party and that he had just recently failed in organizing an alternative movement of the left, the *Rassemblement Democratique Révolutionnaire* (RDR) for which Camus himself had campaigned. A practical question also implicitly divided them: the issue was not simply whether to support or oppose the communists; it was rather how nonaligned intellectuals should act to foster a progressive politics in postwar France where the communist party polled about 20 percent of the vote and received support from much of the working class, and where a democratic socialist alternative to the communists was seemingly lacking. Each answered the question differently and here lay the real source of their conflict.

As a self-styled revolutionary, Sartre took a "realistic" position. He believed "engagement" was always necessary and progressive politics impossible without the Communist party. The Soviet Union was seen by him as, for better or worse, the only nation identifying itself

Albert Camus in trench coat

ideologically with revolution, and, if only for this reason, Sartre endowed it with a certain "privilege" in the Cold War. It was a strange position for a "realist" to take, however, since the Soviet Union had not pursued a genuinely revolutionary course since 1923. As a consequence, even while seeking to foster militancy among the working class, Sartre never specified how the U.S.S.R. or its vassal party in France was furthering this goal. Raymond Aron was correct when he wrote that "the philosopher of liberty never managed, or resigned himself, to see communism as it is."[10]

Camus surely had more foresight than Sartre in seeing communism as a moral obstacle for socialism. He stood on principle, and withdrew his support for UNESCO in 1952 when Franco's Spain became a member. He protested the bloody suppression of the 1953 uprising by workers in East Berlin, but he also signed petitions calling for the release of the Rosenbergs who had been convicted as Soviet spies and sentenced to death in the United States. He actually longed for a genuinely republican front, a coalition capable of opposing both Gaullism and communism, and he had received approval for such a venture from the liberal socialist group around François Bondy and his journal Les Preuves. But, no mass base for such a project existed in France. The unwillingness of Camus to deal with the communists left him without any practical plan for implementing a democratic agenda in the France of his time.

Neither the rebel Camus nor the revolutionary Sartre could offer a coherent theory of "engagement" or an adequate response for the political problems of their epoch. Both found themselves unable to connect their principles with political practice. Admirers of both Camus and Sartre still argue about who "won" the debate. But there were no winners—only losers.

Both men hardened their positions over time. Sartre gradually grew disgusted with the Soviet Union and transferred his allegiance first to the dictatorial Communist regimes of Cuba and then to Red China. One of the greatest intellectuals of the century, in this way, evermore surely lost his political credibility. As for Camus, whatever the popularity of his theory following the collapse of communism in 1989, the 1950s found him isolated, theoretically paralyzed, and unable to identify with one side or the other on the most explosive political issue faced by the Fourth Republic: Algerian independence.

8

THE ALGERIAN WAR

IN THE WINTER OF 1953, FOLLOWING THE DEBATE
with Sartre, Camus visited the Sahara. Then he went to
Holland, Greece, and back to Algeria. It was a time of
restlessness and yet another bout with writer's block. But,
from his depression and anxiety, he put together a
chiseled little collection of essays and travel notes entitled
Summer (*L'Eté*), which he published in 1954. It begins
with the following lines from "The Minotaur":

There are no more deserts. There are no more islands. Yet one still
feels the need of them. To understand this world, one must
sometimes turn away from it; to serve men better, one must briefly
hold them at a distance.[1]

The essays of *Summer*, most of them short, were written
over the years. They reiterate his contempt for any philosophy of history, his suspicions about progress, and his
rejection of force as a means of resolving conflict. Camus
saw himself getting older. Solidarity makes itself felt again.
He now subtly shifts from rebellion to the struggle against
aging and the finality of death:

In the evening, in the fiercely lit cafés where I sought refuge, I read my age on faces I recognized without knowing their names. All I knew was that these men had been young when I was, and that now they were young no longer.[2]

Solidarity cannot compensate for the certainty of impending death or the sense of loss expressed by Camus in his depiction of "towns without a past." But there is also the physical sensuality of "The Sea Close By," which expresses the lure of the Mediterranean or his embrace of a "will to live without refusing anything life offers." However, a hint of bitterness remains. Camus reveals his doubts concerning the ability of an artist to communicate with the public and criticizes the Parisian intelligentsia, which he likens to pirhanhas. He writes in "The Enigma":

No man can say what he is. But sometimes he can say what he is not. Everyone wants the man who is still searching to have already reached his conclusions.

Summer had nothing political about it. This collection of essays and travel notes revealed the "invincible summer," that Camus carried in his heart, and which is stronger than the winter of discontent he had experienced in his battle with Sartre. Ironically, however, the book appeared precisely at the time the Algerian Revolution broke out.

No other event would test Camus in the same way. Years of French economic exploitation and racism, lack of political rights for Arabs in Algeria, and religious intolerance for Islam had produced a bloody uprising led by the National Liberation Front (FLN). As a French Algerian, a *pied-noir*, Camus could identify with this response against oppression that began with the conquest of the colony in 1830. As a French citizen, however, he was also

The entrance to the Casbah, the Arab quarter in Algiers

An oasis in the Sahara desert in Algeria

appalled by the terrorist tactics used by Arabs against Europeans in a genuine war for independence. He could take neither side and condemned those with easy solutions.

Camus publicly supported only one politician in postwar France: Pierre Mendès-France. A hero of the antifascist resistance, an anticommunist and a leader of the Socialist party,[3] his liberal minority government of 1954 remained in power less than a year. He withdrew France from Vietnam, provided Tunisia with gradual independence, and sought to disentangle France from Algeria as well. But his policy received support from neither the right, which was intent on maintaining the French Empire, or the left with its insistence on immediate independence for Algeria.

Algeria was the jewel in the crown of the French Empire. Even moderates believed its loss would destroy France as a major power. Mendès-France was pressured by the followers of de Gaulle to put down the mass-based uprisings of 1954. While holding out offers of economic reform, Mendès-France sent in French troops to support the reactionary governor of Algeria, Jacques Soustelle, who had declared martial law. European sections, mostly white, were sequestered with troops and barbed wire from the native and non white areas. The FLN meanwhile gained support in the impoverished Muslim countryside as it became apparent that the reforms were too little and too late. Mendès-France tried to negotiate and offered free elections, but his government fell before any attempt could be made to realize his promises. A vicious cycle began increased repression in which brought about new acts of terror.

Malraux stood with de Gaulle, Sartre and Jeanson siding with the FLN,[4] while Camus associated himself with Mendès-France. Camus' love for Algeria had always been obvious in his writing, but he now feared Arab fanatics, especially since his mother and uncle fled to

France after an Arab neighbor was stabbed. He started writing a bi-weekly column on Algeria for *L'Express*, a liberal magazine owned by Jean-Jacques Servan-Schreiber, that supported Mendès-France. In its pages, Camus condemned the violence on both sides.

Camus wished to identify with the republican legacy of France and the desire for Algerian self-determination at the same time. He echoed the calls of Mendès-France for a cease-fire, negotiations leading to free elections, and the extension of French citizenship to Algerians. He opposed independence for Algeria, although he supported immediate autonomy for the colony within the French Empire.

Mendès-France resigned in 1955 rather than sacrifice his policy on Algeria or his vision of domestic socialist reform. Camus clung to the former premier's views and he had only contempt for the French far right who were intent on France keeping Algeria at any cost. But he also feared the authoritarian tendencies of the FLN and stood apart from those, like Sartre, who supported Algerian independence. Attitudes only hardened as the violence grew worse.

The Algerian question brought down the Fourth Republic. In 1958, General de Gaulle was called in to form a new Fifth Republic and resolve the crisis. Granted extraordinary presidential power, he turned against his far right-wing supporters and purged the military of reactionary forces. Once the army was under control, France was able to grant Algeria its independence in 1962. Neither the right nor the left, however, could have foreseen such a set of developments in 1954. Their responses to Camus were subsequently entirely predictable. Both sides seemed to agree: the great moralist could not make a simple political judgment.

★ ★ ★ ★ ★

The Fall (*La Chute*) is the most beautiful and the most difficult of all the writings by Camus. It forms a third cycle of works along with *Summer* and *Exile and the Kingdom (L' Exil et le Royaume)*. All were conceived around the same time and, in fact, *The Fall* was originally intended for inclusion in *Exile and the Kingdom*. But the story became long and was published as an independent work in 1956. The absence of Algeria and the sun, for the first time in any of Camus' novels, provides a sense of the dreary hell in which the main character finds himself.[5]

Jean-Baptiste Clamence, the main character, is an "empty prophet for shabby times."[6] Once a lawyer and now a resident of Amsterdam, which Camus had visited for a few days in 1954, he holds court in a tawdry sailors bar named The Mexico City, where he supposedly devotes himself to defending the lowly and the insulted. He even helps blind people cross the street. He has left his successful law practice and comfortable bourgeois existence because he once witnessed a young woman drowning herself and found himself either unwilling or unable to help. This recurring memory produced his "fall" from respectability and—presumably—grace.

His culpability is at issue along with his apparent inability to make a judgment. And so, in order not to be judged by others, Clamence creates his own trial and judges himself. The action unfolds through his confession and Camus himself provided a summary of the novel:

The man who speaks in The Fall *delivers himself of a calculated confession. Exiled in Amsterdam in a city of canals and cold light, where he plays the hermit and the prophet, this former attorney waits for willing listeners in a shady bar.*

He has a modern heart, which means that he can't stand being judged. Thus, he hastens to try himself but does it so as better to judge others. The mirror into which he looks will finally be held out to others.

Where does the confession begin, where the accusation? Is this a man who speaks in this book putting himself on trial, or his era on trial? Is he a particular case, or the man of the day? There is, in any case, a sole truth in this studied play of mirrors: pain and what it promises.[7]

   The Fall is a parable about judgment. In fact, Camus originally had considered calling it Judgment or The Last Judgment. Clamence is superficially sincere in the tale he tells. But his "authenticity" is little more than a sophisticated ploy to escape judgment.[8] His confession reveals a desire for domination and he says as much: "The essential is being able to permit oneself anything, even if, from time to time, one has to profess vociferously one's own infamy."[9]

   Intentions and consequences are again at cross-purposes. Law cannot bridge the divorce between them inherent in an absurd existence. His most nihilistic fantasies are insidiously rationalized by identifying them with those of humanity at large. The trial becomes a farce.

   Camus noted in his diary that "according to the Chinese, empires on the verge of collapse have very many laws."[10] *The Fall* reflects a Europe plagued by disillusionment and uncertainty in the aftermath of World War II, and perhaps this was a reason for the great commercial success of the novel. The world of Clamence is one of bombed-out cities, uncertainty, and a guilt born of living in a "bourgeois hell." He, like his comrades, who suffered through two wars in thirty years, is an "exile without a kingdom."[11]

   Clamence is a portrait of "all and no one." It makes sense then that he should incarnate traits of both Camus and Sartre. His moralism and amorous conquests are references to the public persona of his creator. But the satirical references to Sartre are far more scathing. The character also portrays the uncertain state of mind into which Camus' quarrels with friends and the Algerian events had thrown him.[12] Thus, Clamence can say,

I've lost that lucidity to which my friends used to enjoy paying respects. I say "my friends," moreover as a convention. I have no more friends. I have nothing but accomplices. To make up for this, their number has increased; they are the whole human race. And within the human race, you first of all.[13]

Camus surely sought to exert his revenge on Sartre with this novel. What he had seemingly lost on the battlefield of philosophy, he would now recover by fighting on a different terrain. He would reply satirically through art in the same way as his character, by "exposing himself [and] thereby removing himself from the judgment of others."[14] A caricature of Sartre, who incarnates many of the failings attributed to Camus, Clamence becomes the person who can finally win the approval of the "engaged" intellectuals in the cafés of Paris.

But revenge is never all that sweet. The novel has not maintained its popularity for its criticisms of Sartre and the left-wing literati. Its relevance rests instead on the willingness of Camus to confront a more general concern about the nature of action and the connection between authenticity and inauthenticity. The inability to connect intentions with consequences, which dominates the work, extends to every notion of ethics. The novel potentially undermines the very possibility of developing a moral code of conduct with a political intent. And there lies its greatness. *The Fall* is one of those very few works where the power of the artistic imagination calls into question the values held dear by the author himself.

The rebel now totters on the reef of insincerity. Absolutes have been undercut and rational dialogue shows its limits. An ethical code of conduct can now only rest on a prerational faith in morality, which is what led many to consider the novel in religious terms and even speculate about the author embracing Christianity. There is certainly enough religious imagery in the novel and its basic issues are often framed in Christian terms. But such imagery and motifs occur in all of Camus' work and, in keeping with the strange logic of the novel, Clamence can seek repentence only because he knows it is never forthcoming.

The Fall does not constitute a break with Camus' earlier conception of the absurd, his concern with solidarity, or even the themes of his dissertation. The irony of the novel undermines the cynicism its main character extolls. Camus is unwilling to surrender the problem of morality. Creation still remains open to "correction."

9
THE NOBEL PRIZE

SISYPHUS HAD GROWN MORE MODEST. CAMUS JOINED
many of his critics such as Breton and Sartre in supporting the right of French conscientious objectors to
refuse active military duty in Algeria. In 1957 his
"Reflections on the Guillotine" appeared. It described a
story supposedly told by his father who had initially
applauded the execution of a man indicted for murdering
his own family, but then fell violently sick after
witnessing the scene. Camus came to the aid of young
Muslims condemned to death for acts of terrorism. His
principal political concern now became the contestation
of arbitrary power by the state and the defense of *all*
individuals condemned for their beliefs. He was strident
in his denunciations of the Soviet Union for its
suppression of the Hungarian uprising of 1956. His critics
snickered: they identified his politics with those of the
Red Cross.

★ ★ ★ ★ ★

There was no reason for Camus to feel ashamed. But the
"extreme situation" weighed upon him. He grew ever

more introspective and, in the years leading up to his death, considered himself increasingly isolated. All his works from this final period of his life, in fact, evidence a certain inward turn. Catholic critics convinced of his impending conversion now squared off against those who insisted he had never questioned his secularism. Nothing suggests that Camus was ready for a public conversion although his respect remained for what he considered the sacred. This tension, in fact, unifies the collection of short stories published in 1957 under the title *Exile and the Kingdom.*

The book was not a popular success. It sparked little controversy except perhaps among Catholics like Mauriac, and it has also generally been neglected by critics in comparison with his other works. And basically for good reasons. The stories deal with relevant issues: women's liberation, terrorism, class war, the role of the artist, and religious ideas. But there is no clear delineation of how they are consituted or their social implications. Camus deals with these matters in terms of their personal, existential relevance while their concrete import remains shrouded in metaphysics or myth. Each story deals with a different form of exile. Each resolves its conflicts inwardly, outside the political realm, and exhibits the longings that inspired the religious atheism of Camus' youth.

Exile and the Kingdom begins with the tale, "The Adulterous Woman," which shows how nature can have a spiritual significance. A bourgeois woman of middle age, stifled and unattractive, betrays her conservative husband by surrendering to a pantheistic impulse and experiencing an orgasm in the desert night. She feels a new form of freedom as "the whole sky stretched out over her, fallen on her back on the cold earth."[1] But then she returns to her husband and her previous life. She tells him nothing. There is no reason to think that she will change her life and ask herself "profound questions" about its meaning.[2] The adultery remains symbolic, and liberation, the exile into the kingdom of nature, is momentary and purely subjective.

"The Renegade" takes place during a single day. At its core is the soliloquy of a priest, now a slave, whose tongue has been cut out by the fierce tribes of the Taghaza whom he previously sought to proselytize. Instead, however, he is converted, and he thinks about his conversion to the religion of their cruel and merciless god as he sits in the desert waiting to ambush his successor at the parish. He kills the man; afterward, however, he wonders, "Suppose I am mistaken again!" Doubt undercuts the affirmation of an absolute, and when the priest stretches out his hand in a plea for redemption, he is forced to consider that "death too is cool and its shadow hides no god."[3]

Exiled from the kingdom of the world, imprisoned within himself, the existential anguish of the renegade is juxtaposed against the solidarity highlighted in "The Silent Men," which portrays workers in a barrel factory returning to their jobs after an unsuccessful strike. A pledge is taken not to speak to the boss, and the sense of solidarity among the workers reappears. Class consciousness and a more universal feeling of compassion conflict, however, when a worker's child falls ill. Unfortunately, the implications of this contradiction are never played out. The main character who keeps his word, a worker named Yvars, feels pangs of guilt on the way home although he is at one with his family when he finally returns from work. Conflicts in which individuals are exiled from one another in society are never reconciled other than in the private realm, which only compounds the original problem.

Cultures are estranged from one another as surely as classes in the next story. "L'Hote," which can mean both the guest and the host, is about a white schoolmaster who is placed in charge of an Arab arrested for murder whom he must take to the village for execution. The teacher, who cannot speak the language of the Arab, feels a growing sympathy for his prisoner. And so, when they reach a fork in the road, he sets him free. The Arab, however, walks calmly toward the village. The settler and the Arab do not speak the same language either concretely or metaphorically. Even good will is of no use in creating a common ground. An apolitical inner transformation of both the Arab and the French people rather than a purely political solution is the only way, this story suggests, of resolving the conflict between France and Algeria or, in a broader sense, master and slave.

Exile and the Kingdom was dedicated to Francine, the wife of Camus, who had suffered a nervous breakdown during the summer of 1953. His infidelities and refusal to break definitively with Maria Casarès were apparently among the causes. Camus was grief stricken and concerned about the effect of the disintegrating marriage upon his children. But he refused to change his ways. Camus needed to seduce even as he felt the need for stability. This conflict underpins "The Artist at Work," the longest story in the collection. For the work, Camus used his personal relationship with Francine as a model. The narrative concerns Jonas, an artist unable to create. Expectation produces writer's bloc, seductions produce guilt, time is wasted as anxiety increases, and public fame consumes him. Surely in oblique reference to the political criticisms directed against him, Camus wrote that "his star decidedly protected Jonas, who could thus, without suffering in his conscience, combine the certainties of remembering and the comforts of forgetting."[4] The character vacillates. Nothing is resolved when the story ends. It is not even certain whether Jonas dies or not. The artist is apparently not merely exiled from his public and his family, but from life itself, even as he has real work to do as well as a public to serve.

"The Growing Stone," is the last story in the volume and the most complex. The setting is the Island of Iguape where the French engineer, D'Arrest, becomes friendly with Coq, a black cook on a ship, who had been saved from drowning when it was wrecked in a storm. Coq considered his rescue a miracle and vowed he would carry a heavy stone and lay it at the feet of the Virgin during a religious festival. There is reference to Calvary and, when D'Arrest picks up the stone after Coq stumbles, to the image of Simon carrying the cross for Christ as well. This story is connected to another in which a statue of Christ floated to shore following a different shipwreck. Every year the citizens take chips from it in a ceremony marking their happiness and, every year, the stone regenerates.

Religious metaphors and spiritual forms of solidarity are central in these works. Ignoring them in order to depict the worldview of Camus in antireligious terms is illegitimate.[5] Nor does it make sense simply to pit the scientific reason of the engineer against the genuinely religious feelings of Coq and others in the village. There is a place for both in the thinking of Camus and a place as well for different forms of spiritual experience. In "The Growing Stone" there is a breaking out of the prison of modernity and a "reenchantment of the world."

Such were the concerns of Camus when, in 1957, he was awarded the Nobel prize. He was among the youngest ever so honored for literature and, again and again, he emphasized that he would have voted for Malraux. His acceptance speech was a masterpiece of lyricism and modesty. Here, in a few pages, Camus reiterates the themes of his career and the liberal values to which he dedicated his life. He defends his position on Algeria and denounces terror in all its forms. He also speaks of art and the necessary independence of the artist. Many of his claims are, as usual, philosophically

Camus in Sweden accepting the Nobel prize for literature

questionable and even contradictory. Nevertheless, there is a profound sincerity evident when he says,

To me art is not a solitary delight. It is a means of stirring the greatest number of men by providing them with a privileged image of our common joys and woes. . . The artist fashions himself in that ceaseless oscillation from himself to others, midway between the beauty he cannot do without and the community from which he cannot tear himself. This is why artists scorn nothing. They force themselves to understand instead of judging.

Camus was undoubtedly thrilled by the honor of receiving the Nobel Prize. But what should have been the greatest joy of his literary career unfortunately generated new criticisms and bitterness. Mauriac praised him. But *Humanité*, the newspaper of the Communist party, called Camus the "philosopher of abstract freedom," while Pascal Pia, now close to Sartre, sarcastically labeled him a "secular saint in the service of an anachronistic humanism." Other critics were even less charitable. Some even suggested that the award reflected the fact that Camus no longer had anything to say: he had become a classic.[6]

Camus was plunged into depression. Again he turned to the theater. In 1958 he produced a new version of *The Possessed* (*Les Possedés*) by Dostoyevsky and translated *Timon of Athens* by Shakespeare, which deals with a man deserted by his friends and labeled an enemy of the public. The choice of subject matter reflected his mood. He sought an exit. Camus embarked on new love affairs. Restlessness plagued him. He moved back and forth between Paris and a new house, which he bought in Lourmarin, and traveled to Greece with Maria Casarès. Nothing worked.

Perhaps it was to make sense of his life, his accomplishments no less than his failings, that he began his last novel, *The First Man (Le Premiér Homme)* which was

Camus in his editor's office with copies of his many literary works

published in 1994. The trick lies in transforming his autobiography, the story of a celebrity, into fiction. With his use of the third person, Camus is successful. In this work he finally comes to terms with his father and his senseless death in World War I, as well as with his mother for whom "nothing was left, neither in her nor in this house, of that man who was consumed by a cosmic fire and of whom there remained only a memory as imperceptible as the ashes of a butterfly wing incinerated in a forest fire."[7]

The First Man is a novel of discovery in which Camus tells of his family and of the world they experienced. There are few novels in which poverty is presented with such clarity, such sobriety, such compassion, such anger, and such a lack of bitterness. Camus mixes insight into its brutality with the occasional moments of solidarity and honor it generates. Camus wrote:

The cast of The Dispossessed *with Camus (seated center), who wrote the dramatic adaptation of the novel by Dostoyesky*

To begin with, poor people's memory is less nourished than that of the rich; it has fewer landmarks in space because they seldom leave the place where they live, and fewer reference points in time throughout lives that are gray and featureless. Of course there is the memory of the heart that they say is the surest kind, but the heart wears out with sorrow and labor, it forgets sooner under the weight of fatigue. Remembrance of things past is just for the rich. For the poor it only marks the faint traces on the path to death.[8]

Camus tells of his childhood friends, of his mother's loneliness, of the irrelevance of religion, of Louis Germain and Grenier. But he also tells of the founding of Algeria, the diseases and the terrible hardships undergone by the settlers, as well as personal experiences at school and at home. There is a sense of the racism as well as the conflict between the *pied-noirs* and the Algerians.

Camus is often at the height of his powers. But the novel is ultimately unfinished and uneven. Undeveloped impressions are combined with historical descriptions and lyrical recollections of awe-inspiring power, like the settlement of Algiers by the French pioneers of 1849.[9] Sometimes the existential insight merges with personal rumination and historical sweep. The following relatively long excerpt is worth quoting:

Yes, how they died! How they were still dying! In silence and away from everything, as his father had died in an incomprehensible tragedy far from his native land, after a life without a single free choice—from the orphanage to the hospital, the inevitable marriage along the way, a life that grew around him, in spite of him; until the war killed and buried him; from then and forever unknown to his people and his son, he too was returned to that immense oblivion that was the ultimate homeland of the men of his people, the final destination of a life that began without roots—and so many reports in the libraries of the time about the use of foundlings for this country's settlements, yes, all these found and lost children who built transient towns in order to die forever in themselves and in others.[10]

Camus wished "the book should be heavy with things and flesh."[11] And it is. It exhibits a sensual and even a tactile quality. There are descriptions of being whipped by his grandmother and of swimming with his friends. It speaks of "the curse of work so stupid you could weep and so interminably monotonous that it made the days too long and, at the same time, life too short."[12] The book gives a sense of the way in which the child, Camus, grew into an adolescent, and the manner in which early success in school "uprooted him from the warm and innocent world of the poor—a world closed in on itself like an island in the society."[13] There are interesting attempts to untangle his mixed feelings about Algeria and France along with a willingness to experiment with time.

The First Man offered little that was really new, however, when it appeared posthumously in 1994. Its themes are those elaborated in his essays: physical pleasure, the sun, the sea, and death. But the novel would have looked very different had Camus lived. His notes reveal passages intent on describing how "of 600 settlers sent in 1831, 150 died in their tents. Hence the great number of orphanages in Algeria," or of a "lynching scene: four Arabs thrown off the Kassour," or a "history of the *Combat* movement," or—in a very different vein, of "what he wanted most in the world, which was for his mother to read everything that was his life and his being, [but] that was impossible. His love, his only love, would be forever speechless."[14]

The First Man remains a fragment. And perhaps that is only fitting. This autobiographical manuscript was an attempt to preserve the real, the lived life, in art. No life is ever lived to completion and again, it is only fitting that this work should have remained incomplete. In any event, the critics were surely wrong. Camus was not finished as a writer. This last posthumous novel gives a taste of what might have been and also what was lost when he died in a car crash while en route from Lourmarin to Paris on January 4, 1960 at the age of forty-six.

10
AFTERWORD

ALBERT CAMUS WAS A WONDERFUL NOVELIST, AMONG
the most important of the twentieth century, who merged
the classicism of France with the sensibility of the Mediterranean. Camus affirmed the lived moment and, without surrendering the enlightenment ideals of "lucidity"
or common sense, he looked to Greece and North Africa
with their myths, their beauty and nature, their notions of
balance and proportion, their preoccupation with wis-
dom and fate. His works also express a sensual quality
sadly lacking in those of the most prominent existentialists, and he was one of the very few intellectuals of his
era preoccupied with happiness.

Camus prized honesty and the moment in which an
individual recognizes his or her position in the world. His
thought developed over time. It began with the individual and extended to the community; it moved from
existential responsibility to solidarity with others. There is
a logic to his intellectual development. The earlier
philosophical concerns remained with him until the end.
The absurd and its relativism; the limits of reason and the

foibles of passion; resistance and responsibility; rebellion and the arrogance of utopian thinking; human dignity and the lived life of the individual.

These themes and values are part of all of his works. Sisyphus, Mersault, Rieux, and the rest all exhibit a mixture of skepticism and tolerance, lucidity and courage, a sense of responsibility and a willingness to learn. They would surely have liked each other. The others, the less sympathetic characters like Caligula and Clamence, lacked values such as these. Their absence marks their presence. Camus might well have been speaking of himself when he wrote that "a man's work is nothing but this slow trek to rediscover, through the detours of art, those two or three great and simple images in whose presence his heart first opened."[1]

★ ★ ★ ★ ★

Camus was a moralist in keeping with a great tradition of French intellectual thought reaching back to Montaigne and Pascal. He had little use for the metaphysical and sought the concrete. A healthy skepticism lay at the core of his thinking. But, it was always somehow combined with an almost naive compassion for the oppressed and exploited. Indeed, this delicate balance inspires his conception of art and its political role

For a revolutionary work is not one that glorifies victories and conquests, but one that brings to light the Revolution's most painful conflicts. The more painful the conflicts, the greater their effect. The militant too quickly convinced is to the true revolutionary what the bigot is to a mystic. For the grandeur of a faith can be measured by the doubts it inspires."[2]

Themes of a religious sort were present in the work of Camus from the very beginning. The titles of his last books, *The Fall* and *Exile and the Kingdom*, speak for themselves and the "absurd" is ultimately defined by religious longing as well as the absence of God. But, whatever his spiritual inclinations, the dogma of organized religion appealed to him as little as what had become the catechism of Marxism. The absurd is the reality with which each individual has to deal. That is why murder and suicide are, for him, pressing issues. They are flip sides of the same coin. The only moral justification for murder is the willingness to offer one's own life in exchange or, in short, suicide. Both forms of action, however, surrender to the absurd insofar as they deny dialogue, solidarity, human dignity, and the possibility of giving meaning to a meaningless world. Whether this moral stance articulated by Camus, which links murder with suicide, actually makes either philosophical or political sense is questionable. Members of movements engaged in genuine conflicts cannot make these kind of assumptions while, for the incurably sick and bedridden, human dignity and their happiness is perhaps best served by giving them the right to die.

None of this, however, really concerns Camus. His aim is making people face themselves and, like Sartre, take responsibility for their actions. Camus contests the way in which anonymous masses were murdered by equally anonymous bureaucrats intent on "obeying orders." His response is an ethic built on certain postulates about reasonable human interaction. His deep pessimism evidenced in his preoccupation with death and the absence of meaning is thus complemented by an abiding optimism based on a belief in human decency and the power to learn. Art must reflect this peculiar balance between pessimism and optimism. Thus, Camus could write:

...impossibility for man to despair utterly. Conclusion: any literature of despair represents but an extreme case and not the most significant. The remarkable thing in man is not that he despairs, but

that he overcomes or forgets despair. A literature of despair will never be universal. Universal literature cannot stop at despair; not at optimism either: just reverse the reasoning; it must merely take despair into account.[3]

Camus never wallowed in the absurd. He knew its un-critical acceptance, the effect of its logic in political affairs, would turn individuals into the playthings of arbitrary whims and utopian schemes. Experiencing the absurd, for him, is merely a first step. Contesting it from the stand-point of "lucidity" and solidarity is the real goal. A "rebel-lion," in this way, is needed against the deduction made famous by one of Dostoyevsky's characters: "If God does not exist then everything is permitted."

Such a rebellion, however, contests any unqualified commitment to an all-encompassing revolution let alone an apocalypse. It rests on breaking the identification of freedom with license and, for this reason, Camus saw the need to impose "limits" on action. Only in this way would it become possible to preserve the individual from the clutches of "historical necessity." The denial of "limits" thrusts action into the abyss and, for all the sacrifices undertaken in the name of abolishing it, the absurd appears once again.

Camus remained a man of the left until the end of his life. Liberalism, socialism, and syndicalism combined uneasily in his political theory. It was his preoccupation with the individual, his humanism, which made them compatible. Because the absurd justifies the exercise of arbitrary power, in fact, Camus could contend: "We must serve justice because our condition is unjust, increase happiness and joy because this universe is unhappy. Like-wise, we must not condemn others to death because we have been given the death sentence."[4]

Camus saw through the self-serving excuses for em-ploying terror. He recognized the value of constitutions and civil liberties because they alone protect the individual from the exercise of arbitrary power and enable one to deal with his or her private fate. His worldview called for a coherent connection between means and ends and, perhaps for this very reason, he was never a particularly insightful political analyst. How well he actually understood the institutional dynamics of either fascism or communism remains open to question. And it was the same with imperialism.

Camus was never interested in the nuts and bolts of politics.[5] His substitution of rebellion for revolt skirted the fact that reform is not possible under every regime and revolution can take numerous forms. If he insisted on political engagement only in the "extreme situation," which his emphasis on "Mediterranean moderation" intentionally sought to prevent,[6] he tended to forget that social action is not like a taxicab that can simply be made to stop at any corner. In spite of all this, however, the basic insight of Camus remains valid: only by recognizing the vanity of attempting to change everything is it possible to change some things. This was the sense in which he envisioned a "creation corrected," the title Camus imagined for a never completed final work.

His star shines brighter with the passing of time. He was an activist fearful of power and a genuinely "multicultural" thinker whose inspiration derived from two continents. His liberalism made him identify with the civil rights movement and turned him into an apostle of human rights before the term was invented. His syndicalist sympathies and concern with happiness made him an influence on the cultural radicals of the 1960s and 1970s. His understanding of rebellion anticipated the anticommunist demonstrations of 1989 and his social democratic sympathies speak to the economic inequality of the present.

Albert Camus was an advocate of decency. Values were the weapons with which he fought against the darkness and their depiction in his fascinating novels and exciting plays, luminous essays and pristine aphorisms makes him more than just another great intellectual representative of the past. Camus was the conscience of a bygone age; he remains the conscience of our own as well.

A CHRONOLOGICAL TABLE

1913
Albert Camus is born in Mondovi, Algeria, to Lucien Camus, whose family had settled in Algeria in 1871, and Catherine Sintés, of Spanish origin.

1914
Lucien Camus is killed in the Battle of the Marne during World War I. Catherine Sintés moves into her grandmother's apartment in the working-class Belcourt neighborhood of Algiers.

1918-1923
Albert attends primary school. Meets Louis Germain.

1924-1930.
As a scholarship student, studies at the *Lycée* of Algiers. Lives at the home of his uncle Gustave Acault, and meets Jean Grenier.

1930
Experiences first attack of tuberculosis and studies are interrupted. Supports himself at various odd jobs.

1931
Creation of the Spanish republic.

1932
Receives his baccalaureate. Works with Algerian Federation of Young Socialists.

1933
Adolf Hitler takes power in Germany. Camus enters the University of Algiers.

1934
Camus marries Simone Hié. Fascist riots in Paris. Joins the Communist party and is entrusted with propaganda work among the Muslims.

1935
Pierre Laval is invited to Moscow. Camus' disillusionment with the Communist party begins. Founds the *Theatre du Travail*. Works as an actor, director, and playwright.

1936
Electoral victory of the Popular Front. Camus receives his university degree in philosophy with the thesis "*Christian Metaphysics and Neoplatonism.*" Travels in Central Europe. Marriage to Simone Hié breaks up. Civil war in Spain breaks out. Camus produces his play *The Revolt in Asturia.*

1937
Completes *A Happy Death*, which will remain unpublished during his lifetime. The essay collection *The Right Side and the Wrong Side* is published. Supports the Blum-Viollette legislation on mitigating social problems in Algeria. Expulsion from the Communist party. The *Theatre du Travail* becomes the *Theatre de l'Equipe.*

1938
End of the Popular Front. Meets Pascal Pia. Camus becomes a journalist for the *Álger-Républicain.* The Munich Pact is concluded. Camus writes *Caligula.*

1939
World War II begins. The essay collection *Nuptials* is published. Camus reports on the Kabylian famine.

1940

Divorce from Simone Hié is finalized. Second marriage to Francine Faure in Lyon. *Álger-Républicain* is banned and Camus loses his job. He leaves Algeria and Pia gets him an editorial position at *Paris-Soir*. Camus completes *The Stranger*.

1941

Returns to Algeria. Teaches French Studies at a private school and completes *The Myth of Sisyphus*.

1942

Publication of *The Stranger*. Returns to the French town of Chambon-sur-Lignon after an outbreak of tuberculosis. Allied landing in North Africa strands him in southern France. He will remain separated from his wife until the liberation.

1943

Battle of Stalingrad. Publication of *The Myth of Sisyphus*. Becomes an editor at Gallimard, the publishing house, a position he will hold until his death. Joins the French Resistance and moves to Paris. Publication of the first *Letter to a German Friend*.

1944

Allied liberation of France. Meets Jean-Paul Sartre, Simone de Beauvoir, Arthur Koestler, Maurice Merleau-Ponty, and Maria Casarès. *The Misunderstanding* is produced. Publication of the next three *Letters to a German Friend*. Becomes editor of the clandestine newspaper *Combat*.

1945

End of World War II. Birth of the Camus twins: Jean and Catherine. *Caligula* is produced. Camus returns to Algeria where he reports on the brutal repression of anti-imperialist demonstrations in Sétif.

1946

Constitution for the Fourth Republic is ratified. *Neither Victims nor Executioners* is published. Lecture tour of the United States. Controversy with François Mauriac about the punishment of collaborators. Breaks with Merleau-Ponty following a political discussion concerning the Soviet Union.

1947

Publication of *The Plague*. Sartre founds the *Rassemblement Democratique et Revolutionnaire*. Camus condemns the repression of an anti-imperialist revolt in Madagascar.

1948

State of Siege is produced. Fall of the "iron curtain" and beginning of the Cold War. Co-founder of *Groupe de Liason Internationale*.

1949

Lecture tour of South America. *The Just* Assassins is produced. Begins work on *The Rebel*.

1950

New attacks of tuberculosis.

1951

Publication of *The Rebel*. War breaks out in Korea.

1952

Controversy with Sartre. Visits Algeria once again. Resigns from UNESCO when Franco's Spain is admitted to membership. Starts work on the stories for *Exile and the Kingdom* and *The First Man*.

1953

Camus condemns the repression of a workers' revolt in East Berlin. Visits the Sahara.

1954

Summer is published. Camus visits Amsterdam. Intervenes for seven Tunisians condemned to death for their political activities. Beginning of the Algerian War for Independence. Mendès-France elected premier.

1955

Camus becomes a contributor to *L'Express*. Mendès-France government falls.

1956

Publication of *The Fall*. Produces *Requiem for a Nun* by William Faulkner. Soviet repression of the anticommunist uprising in Hungary. Camus appeals for a truce in Algeria. Intervenes in favor of various Algerian liberals and nationalists who have been put under arrest.

1957

Publication of *Exile and the Kingdom* and "Reflections on the Guillotine." *Caligula* is revived. Camus is awarded the Nobel Prize for Literature.

1958

De Gaulle returns to power. The Fifth Republic is established. Camus republishes *The Right Side and the Wrong Side* with a new introduction.

1959

French Minister of Culture, André Malraux, offers Camus artistic control over the *Comedie Française*. Camus refuses. He adapts *The Possessed* by Dostoyevsky and *Timon of Athens* by Shakespeare for the experimental stage. Works full-time on *The First Man*.

1960

Camus is killed in an automobile accident.

1962
Algeria receives independence.

1971
Publication of *A Happy Death.*

1994
Publication of *The First Man.*

SOURCE NOTES

Chapter 1

1. Herbert Lottmann, *Albert Camus: A Biography* (New York, 1979), pg. 8.

2. Albert Camus, "The Right Side and the Wrong Side" in *Lyrical and Critical Essays*, ed. Philip Thody and trans. Ellen Conroy Kennedy (New York, 1968), 27.

3. Albert Camus, *Notebooks*, 2 vols., trans. Justin O'Brien (New York, 1991), I:3.

4. Germaine Brée, *Camus* (New Brunswick, NJ: 1959), 12.

5. Jean Grenier, *Albert Camus: Souvenirs* (Paris, 1968), 13.

6. Patrick Mc Carthy, Camus: *A Critical Study of His Life and Works* (London, 1982), 15.

7. Cited from "Two Letters" appended to Albert Camus, *The First Man*, trans. David Hapgood (New York, 1995), 321.

8. "Grenier's relationship with Camus is often misunderstood...If he had cared more for Grenier, he might have publicized his gratitude less, for it mortified Grenier who saw himself robbed of his own originality and reduced to an appendage of Camus. The postwar Camus-Grenier relationship was full of concealed hypocrisies which lay beyond the master-pupil effusions and by the end Camus was thoroughly sick of him. Meanwhile Grenier fought back by telling everyone that he had done little for Camus, no more than for other students." Ibid., 32ff and passim.

9. Lottman, 46.

10. The debate concerning the religious or secular character of his thought appears in the articles by Thomas L. Hannah, "Albert Camus and the Christian Faith"; Bernard C. Murchland, C.S.C., "Albert Camus: the Dark Night Before the Coming of Grace?"; Henri Peyre, "Camus the Pagan," all of which are included in *Camus: A Collection of Critical Essays* ed. by Germaine Brée (Englewood Cliffs, NJ: 1962), 48-70. Also note the balanced study by Jean Onimus, *Albert Camus and Christianity,* trans. Emmett Parker (Alabama,1970).

Chapter 2

1. Thus, while visiting the Cemetery of El Kettar, he could note: "One solitary geranium, its leaves both pink and red, and a great silent feeling of loss and sadness that teaches us to know the pure and beautiful face of death." Camus, *Notebooks*, I:74.

2. Camus, *Lyrical and Critical Essays*, 14.

3. Ibid., 29.

4. Camus, "Three Interviews," in *Lyrical and Critical Essays*, 358.

5. Camus, *Lyrical and Critical Essays*, 78.

6. Ibid., 104.

7. Camus, *Notebooks,* I:16.

8. Cf. McCarthy, Camus, 55; Guérin, Camus, 16. Other scholars claim that Camus entered the Communist party in 1934 and the least critical mistakenly suggest that he left a year later. Cf. Philip Thody, *Albert Camus 1913–1960* (London, 1961), 5; Brée, *Camus*, 26; also, Lottman, *Albert Camus*, 77ff.

9. Lottman, *Albert Camus*, 147.

10. "Politically, Camus' view was ridiculous. Despite his anti-fascist stand, he had not grasped the nature of the Hitler regime. Not until after the fall of France did he realize that it was especially virulent. Moreover, he chose to ignore that France could not fight Hitler while parading her readiness to negotiate with him. While insisting that he was rejecting fatalism in the name of action, Camus was condemning himself to passivity." McCarthy, Camus, 125.

11. Lottman, Albert Camus, 186ff.

12. Justin O'Brien, "Albert Camus: Militant" in *Camus: A Collection of Critical Essays*, 23.

13. Brée, *Camus*, pg. 35.

Chapter 3

1. Camus, *Notebooks*, I:189.
2. Albert Camus, *The Stranger, trans.* Stuart Gilbert (New York, 1946), 154.

3. There is an irreducible difference between the notion and the experience of the absurd; indeed, "*The Myth of Sisyphus* might be said to aim at giving us this idea, and *The Stranger* at giving us the feeling." Sartre, "An Explication of *The Stranger,*" pg. 114.

4. Camus, *Lyrical and Critical Essays*, 337.

5. Pierre-Georges Castex, *Albert Camus et "L'Etranger"* (Paris, 1965), 123.

6. Albert Camus, *The Myth of Sisyphus and Other Essays,* trans. Justin O'Brien (New York, 1955), v.

7. "I realize that if through science I can seize phenomena and enumerate them, I cannot, for all that, apprehend the world." Ibid., 14.

8. Camus, *The Myth of Sisyphus*, 5.

9. "That nostalgia for unity, that appetite for the absolute illustrates the essential impulse of the human drama. But the fact of that nostalgia's existence does not imply that it is to be immediately satisfied." ibid., 13.

10. Ibid., 40.

11. Ibid.,39.

12. Ibid., 90-1.

13. Camus, *The Myth of Sisyphus*, 75.

14. Roger Quilliot, *The Sea and Prisons: A Commentary On the Life of Albert Camus,* trans. Emmett Parker (Alabama, 1970), 45.

15. Albert Camus, "Caligula" in *Caligula and Three Other Plays*, trans. Stuart Gilbert (New York, 1958), 4.

16. Ibid., 8.

17. Ibid.

18. Ibid., 21.

19. Ibid., 43.

20. Spritzen, *Camus*, 77.

Chapter 4

1. Lottman, 316ff.

2. H. Stuart Hughes, *The Obstructed Path: French Social Thought in the Years of Desperation 1930–1960* (New York, 1968), 155.

3. McCarthy, Camus, 175ff.

4. "Whenever you asked Camus for a favour, he would do it so readily that you never hesitated to ask for another and never in vain. Several of our younger friends also wanted to work

for *Combat*; he took them all in. Opening the paper in the morning was almost like opening our mail. Towards the end of November, athe United States wanted its war effort to be better known in France and invited a dozen reporters to the States. I've never seen Sartre so elated as the day Camus offered him the job of representing *Combat*." Simone deBeauvoir, *The Force of Circumstance*, trans. Richard Howard (New York, 1965) 24.

5. Lev Braun, *Witness of Decline: Albert Camus: Moralist of the Absurd* (New Jersey, 1974), 80.

6. Albert Camus, "Letters to a German Friend" in *Resistance, Rebellion, and Death*, trans. Justin O'Brien (New York, 1960), 3-25.

7. Ibid., 6.

8. ibid.

Chapter 5

1. Published in tandem with *Caligula*, however, it sold better than any other work of Camus until the appearance of *ThePlague*. Cf. Rehbein, *Albert Camus*, 41ff.

2. McCarthy, *Camus*, 190ff.

3. Note the author's preface in Camus, *Caligula and Three Other Plays*, vii.

4. Camus, "The Misunderstanding" in *Caligula and Three Other Plays*, 123.

5. Ibid., 79.

6. Ibid., 123-4.

7. McCarthy, *Camus*, 174ff.

8. Albert Camus, "Letter to Roland Barthes on *The Plague* in *Lyrical and Critical Essays*, 338.

9. Albert Camus, *The Plague*, trans. Stuart Gilbert (New York, 1948), 150.

10. Brian Masters, *Camus* (New Jersy, 1974), 64.

11. Bree, *Camus*, 121.

12. Camus, *The Plague*, 278

13. Camus was as little interested in "realism" as pure formalism. Both were for him symmetrical forms of "nihilism." He was as opposed to merely reproducing the "real" as expelling it in the name of purely aesthetic considerations.Cf. Guérin, *Camus*, 69.

14. Parker, *Albert Camus*, 64.

15. Thody, *Albert Camus*, 102.

16. Camus, "Letter to Roland Barthes," 340.

17. Bree, *Camus*, pgs. 86ff.

18. Parker, *Albert Camus*, 113.

19. Camus, *The Plague*, 226-8.

20. Ibid., 2:10.

Chapter 6

1. Cf. Lottman, *Albert Camus*, 376ff.

2. Mc Carthy, *Camus*, 231.

3. Guérin, *Camus*, 43ff; Parker, *Albert Camus* 93ff; McCarthy, *Camus* 213ff.

4. Note the response to the critical review of the play by Catholic existentialist and politically consevative writer, Gabriel Marcel, entitled "Why Spain??" in Albert Camus "Why Spain?" in *Resistance, Rebellion, and Death*, 75ff.

Chapter 7

1. Albert Camus, *The Rebel*, trans. Anthony Bower (New York, 1954), 5.

2. Ibid., 103.

3. Camus, "The New Mediterranean Culture" (1937) in *Lyrical and Critical Essays*, 197.

4. Louis Patsouras, *Jean Grave and the Anarchist Tradition in France* (New Jersey, 1995), 102ff.

5. Cf. Albert Beguin, "Albert Camus, la revolte et le bonheur" in *Esprit* (April, 1952), 736.

6. Beauvoir, *The Force of Circumstance*, 271.

7. Jean-Paul Sartre, "Reply to Albert Camus" in *Situations*, trans. Benita Eisler (New York, 1965), 54ff.

8. Such exaggerations, which work far more to the disadvantage of Sartre than Camus, are reproduced without taking the immediate political context adequately into account by Paul Johnson, *The Intellectuals* (New York, 1988), 125-151 and Tony Judt, *Past Imperfect: French Intellectuals, 1944–56* (Berkeley, 1992).

9. Guérin, *Camus*, 105.

10. Raymond Aron, *Memoirs: Fifty Years of Political Reflections*, trans. George Holoch (New York, 1990), 330.

Chapter 8

1. Albert Camus, "Summer" in *Lyrical and Critical Essays*, 109.

2. Ibid., 163.

3. Note the superb biography by Jean Lacouture, *Pierre Mendès-France*, trans. George Holoch (New York, 1984), 211ff.

4. Guérin, *Camus*, 163.

5. Brée, *Camus*, 13.

6. Albert Camus, *The Fall*, trans. Justin O'Brien (New York, 1956), 117.

7. Cited in Lottman, *Albert Camus*, 564.

8. Sprintzen, *Camus*, 199.

9. Camus, *The Fall*, 141.

10. Camus, *Notebooks*, 2:247.

11. Gäeton Picon, "Exile and the Kingdom" in *Camus*, 155.

12. McCarthy, *Camus*, 310.

13. Camus, *The Fall*, 73.

14. Lottman, *Albert Camus*, 565.

Chapter 9

1. Albert Camus, *Exile and the Kingdom*, trans. Justin O'Brien (New York, 1958), 33.

2. English Showalter Jr. *Exiles and Strangers: A Reading of Camus's Exile and the Kingdom* (Columbus, Ohio: 1984), 27.

3. Camus, *Exile and the Kingdom*, 53.

4. Ibid., 116.

5. Brée, *Camus*, 132.

6. Lottman, *Camus*, 600ff.

7. Albert Camus, *The First Man*, trans. David Hapgood (New York, 1995), 73

8. Ibid., 80.

9. Ibid., 185ff.

10. Ibid., 193-4.

11. Ibid., 105.

12. Ibid., 270.

13. Ibid., 176.

14. Ibid., 286, 294, 296, 300.

Chapter 10

1. Camus, "Preface of 1958" to *The Right Side and the Wrong Side*, 17.

2. Camus, "Review of Bread and Wine by Ignazio Silone" in *Lyrical and Critical Essays*, 208.

3. Camus, *Notebooks*, 2:112-3.

4. Ibid., 2:99.

5. Every time I hear a political speech or I read those of our leaders, I am horrified at having, for years, heard nothing which sounded human. It is always the same words telling the same lies," ibid., I:48.

6. "One must declare that one is not a revolutionary, but more modestly a reformer. An uncompromising theory of reform. Finally, and *taking everything into consideration*, one may call oneself a rebel." Camus, *Notebook*, 2:214.

INDEX

ABOUT THE AUTHOR

Stephen Eric Bronner, an author and historian, is a professor of political science and comparative literature at Rutgers University. He has written on the history of socialist thought and France and Germany in the twentieth century, as well as biographies of Léon Blum and Rosa Luxemburg. He lives in New York City with his wife Anne.